PORCELAIN

&

POTTERY MARKS

COPYRIGHT 1943

BY

HAZEL HARTMAN
62 WEST 45th STREET
NEW YORK CITY, N. Y.

PRINTED IN THE UNITED STATES

524674

FOR THEIR COOPERATION AND ASSISTANCE
IN COMPILING THIS BOOK, THE PUBLISHER
EXPRESSES HIS APPRECIATION TO

OLIVER and LILLIAN ALLARD

Many people have found the secret of enriching their lives by cultivating a hobby. Some, like President Franklin D. Roosevelt collect stamps, others coins, rare books, old letters and many other interesting items. Among the more exciting hobbies is the collecting of porcelain. Porcelain has a history comparable with the fine arts, and ranks with Rembrandt and Donatellos, as a collectors' joy.

Like many famous artists who went into seclusion, so that no one could determine how they blended their colors, so too, is the earliest recollection of this unusual early porcelain making steeped in secrecy. For hundreds of years, European travelers attempted to get the secret from China, where porcelain was first invented, but were unsuccessful.

The exact origin of porcelain goes back to the 9th century, in China, although the oldest specimens today are attributed to the 10th century. Travellers and tradesmen from Japan, Korea, and faraway Persia, acquired the art of porcelain making, and soon made porcelain of their own. However, it remained a mystery to the rest of the world, until the time of the Mohammedan conquest.

The earliest trace of European true porcelain making goes back to 16th century. An old potter who had lived in Venice, died without passing on the secret of his work. Men and women attempted to make porcelain all during the 16th century but without success. However, it is believed that an Englishman did make some true porcelain in 1671, but there are no specimens of his work in existence. A type of porcelain which we now call "soft paste," was made in St. Cloud, France, during the latter part of the 17th century. It was not until the year 1710, that the true formulae for porcelain was invented. Mr. Böttger, a young man in the employ of the royal house of Saxony was the inventor.

Since all early European porcelain was an attempt to copy the Chinese, these early potters also tried to imitate the Chinese marks. These first pieces were not well-made and the imitations were quite obvious. If one examines these early English, Dutch, or German wares, he will readily note the forged Chinese marks.

Today the unusual beauty of fine porcelain is attaining the popularity it so richly deserves. Eight or ten years ago, there were few collectors of porcelain in this country. Now there are many thousands, and five years from now these thousands will double and even treble. Good taste in home decorations must include a collection of porcelains.

A large proportion of collectors today are people in limited circumstances. Some accumulate very interesting and tasteful collections of miniature pieces, while others specialize in acquiring vases, pitchers, or cups and saucers. Then again, in other homes one may find a combination of good and inferior porcelain. This is like having the proverbial bad apple spoiling the collection. The good pieces are overshadowed by the bad. Many persons will purchase an article just for the maker's mark. Even the best makers produced poor pieces occasionally. Much too frequently people value the factory mark and forget the merit of the individual piece.

It is a common occurrence these days to see crowds attracted by a display of fine china in some shop window. But like diamonds, furniture and rugs, porcelain is an unknown item to most of them. The preparation of a book of marks, with an outline of porcelain manufacturers up to the end of the 19th century is exceedingly necessary. Here, all old china will be identified. This will naturally be of paramount importance to the dealer, collector, and student.

Few dealers know the history of porcelain and the burden of doing intelligent shopping lies on the shoulders of the prospective buyer. It is very important for the amateur collector to shop the second hand stores. Many unusual and valuable opportunities present themselves from time to time. The writer has made some of his best purchases at these little shops, often making a handsome profit.

One need not be an expert to discover unusual treasures. Few second hand dealers know what they actually have, and what is more important, know less about the true value of these pieces. Very often you will find articles marked ridiculously low, while others are marked much above their true value. It is not unusual to see cheap Dresden marked $15 when their true worth is less than $1. Too frequently, dealers as well as buyers set their prices on articles in view of their factory mark alone. The mere stamp of an old

Worcester or Dresden mark is not sufficient to make an item valuable. The experienced buyer will use his good taste, and combine the origin of the piece with its artistic beauty, and set his own figure as to value.

When making a purchase it is very important to determine whether the item is porcelain or pottery, whether it be soft paste or hard. By holding the article to the light and seeing the outline of your hand you can then tell that this is porcelain. Should this item be made of a thick substance, then a stronger light is necessary. The next step is to consult your book of marks to identify the maker and age, you can then determine its value. Although this book contains a nearly complete index of marks up to the 20th century that are available today, there are new marks that are constantly being discovered. The marks contained in this book are up to the 20th century only.

You must keep in mind the fact that antiquity does not add to the value of any article, unless it has historical or artistic value aside from its age. You must realize that ofttimes a beautiful work originating from an unknown artist or factory is ofttimes valued higher than a poor specimen of a famous artist or recognized factory. I have often seen and read about paintings and other works of art bringing tremendous prices solely because of the name of the artist. Yet, I am sure that were the artist alive today he would be the first to destroy this work as an inferior canvas. Only recently the major newspapers carried the story of a living American painter, who very openly admitted that he would prefer to destroy many of his paintings because he realized that they were inferior. However, these same paintings brought a high price, only because of the name and reputation of the artist.

The author takes it upon himself to submit some DON'TS for the prospective buyer of porcelain.

DON'T purchase any article simply because of the reputation of the factory mark. Bad porcelain is still bad regardless of the mark it bears.

DON'T purchase broken or poorly mended pieces just because they are marked reasonably. Very often the cost of repairing brings the price up to what a perfect piece would cost.

DON'T purchase old pieces just for the sake of antiquity. It must have more than age to be desirable. Always remember that beauty is the first requisite of every good collector. A beautiful piece made by an unknown is worth more than a less attractive piece from a well-known factory.

The association and possession of beautiful and artistic objects has a good effect on the character and does influence individuals. It brings about a better understanding among people, since they can recognize the abilities and give credit for them to groups who are scattered over the entire globe. The arts are written into the histories of every country. Some excel in music, others in paintings, others literature. Each country is famous for something else. In studying world history you will find that the entire Chinese history is woven into its porcelain. Likewise, on the porcelains of Europeans, you will find their respective histories engraved for eternity to decipher. One of the best examples is English porcelain, where one can see the English Toby jugs of famous Englishmen, even to the modern greats of history. Whenever an important personage appears on the horizon a toby jug commemorates his personality. President Wilson and many of the allied Generals of the World War were used as models. At present, you can purchase Toby jugs of Churchill and Chamberlain.

There was a time from early 1870 to 1900 when potters of every country made porcelain of Japanese styles and character. This was when Japan was the popular and newest country for tourists to visit.

The actual story of European porcelain begins about 200 years ago. At that time only royalty and the extremely wealthy were able to afford china since it had to be brought from the Orient. Those less fortunate had to be content with coarse pottery or pewter. The very poor used wooden utensils or the very coarsest of pottery. The poorest home today takes their porcelain service for granted, few of us realize the hardships and disappointments that had to be overcome, in order to pass this important invention on to us.

Great care was taken to assure the complete secrecy of this great invention. Prices were kept very high and the styles were usually copied from the Chinese. However, as more and more factories were opened, prices became lower and soon the middle class people were able to afford this luxury. It did not take long before the very poor were also able to purchase china dishes. Today most European countries have specially equipped laboratories to create new ideas and styles in this great art.

Secrecy is still all important, and only old and trusted employees are permitted to work on the new designs and new principles of enameling.

When F. de Medici died in 1587 the manufacture of porcelain in Europe was halted. No one knew how to continue this art. Another death that seemed to stop this work of art was when a Mr. Poterat passed away in Rouen. He had been able to manufacture a type of glassy porcelain that had yellowish color.

It was not until 1710 that a young man named Böttcher or Bötger invented porcelain quite by accident. There are many stories told of the manner of his important discovery, but none are, or can be true. However, he did discover the art of making true porcelain. Mr. Bötger was then employed as an alchemist under the patronage of Augustus of Saxony. When the true significance of this discovery became known he was seized with his workers and held at a fortress in Meissen. They were so closely guarded that you could almost call them prisoners. Daily they were forced to swear that they would not divulge the secret. Even the common workmen who gathered the kaolin, (raw clay) were deaf and dumb. Every precaution was taken to prevent this secret from leaking out. On the walls of the fortress were signs which read "Secrecy to Death."

Some of these men eventually escaped and started factories under the protection of royal owners. However the factory at Meissen retained the original secret and it was not until Napoleon over-ran Germany, that the King gave permission to the manager of the factory to forswear his oath and reveal the formula to the manager of Napoleon's factory at Sevres.

No pottery made by any European could compare with the Chinese until Mr. Bötger of Saxony invented the true porcelain. Another type had been introduced in France, and

still another in England. The English had used an entirely
new base made of ground bone in the clay which produced
a fine white and translucent finish. During the beginning of
the 19th century France and Germany copied the English
method of using ground bone.

Most of the potters copied each other's methods, styles
and designs and in many instances copied the marks. It was
not until the middle of the 19th century that the factories
began to specialize in individuality of design and became
known for definite style in porcelain.

There is a very peculiar story that my readers may find
amusing. The Bötger pieces were offered at a sale at the
Leipzig Fair in 1710 and prices were higher than the original Chinese works. His were forgeries of the Chinese even
to the marks. Strangely enough, though his work was inferior, yet they bring much more money than the original
Chinese pieces whenever they are sold.

Bötger, who died in 1719, lived a short but exciting life.
His workmen were continuously escaping and starting new
factories all over Germany and Austria. An important factory was established in Dresden. The manager had escaped
from the Meissen plant. The best period for the Meissen
works were between 1730 and 1775. The factory was then
under the management of a Mr. Kandler, a very capable
person. The factory enjoyed great popularity, and their
works were exported all over Europe and the near East.
Now, there are hundreds of factories in and around Dresden,
that enjoy great prestige.

Other factories which were established elsewhere in Germany, by ex-workmen of Bötger, who produced similar
works like those of Meissen. They copied each other's styles
and designs. Some were better and some poorer. Among those
that are better in my opinion are the following—Höchst, 1720
— Frankenthal, 1756 — Nymphenburg, 1758 — Fürstenberg,
1746. None, however, enjoyed the reputation of Höchst. This
factory was closed permanently in 1794, when overrun by
Napoleon's armies. The products of the German potters had
begun to deteriorate at the end of the 18th century and the
first advance of German technic started in the early 19th
century. It was discovered that by dipping lace in a solution

of fresh porcelain and then immediately firing it, the thread would burn off, leaving a lacey porcelain product. No other country has given greater scientific study to this art than Germany, especially during the latter part of the 19th century.

Mr. C. Du Paquier, in 1718, employed a workman who had been connected with Bötger. This factory which was located in Vienna, turned out some very beautiful and elaborate decorations in rich colors. These had very heavy gold gildings and magnificent figure paintings. The ruling Austrian family owned the factory which was operated at a loss and was closed in 1864. There are more imitations of so-called (Royal Vienna) than of any other porcelain factory products. The imitations are very poor in gilding, coloring, designs and porcelain. They are rarely hand decorated.

New factories were springing up all over Europe at about that time. Among the better ones were the following: The Royal Copenhagen factory in Copenhagen, established by King Christian II, in 1772. He employed German workmen who copied the Meissen styles. This factory was sold to private individuals in 1867, because of the financial losses it had sustained. This factory has become world famous for its modeling of animals and statuettes.

Another famous factory still in existence, that developed a style of its own was started by Mr. Carlo Ginori. The vases, figures and service were decorated with raised figures, of mythological creations in deep relief. Colors were usually red and gold, although blue was also used. All this against a white background. Collectors have made this one of their favorite items.

A distinctive porcelain factory was established in 1830, by Mr. Moritz Fischer, in Hungary. His early pieces were copied from the Chinese, and he went so far as to use Chinese workmen to decorate them. Another was the factory started by Mr. Zsolnay, who specialized in vases and service. These pieces were highly perforated and richly enamelled. His factory opened in 1885 and is still famous for that type of work.

Mr. Christian Fischer who started a factory in Carlsbad also made very beautiful articles, yet, he too, copied the work of Zsolnay. Pieces from both these factories are highly prized by collectors.

Bernard Palissy is considered the father of French Potters. He experimented for 16 years searching for white
porcelain. He finally gave up the experiment, after losing a
fortune. He did invent what is now known as the Palissy
Ware. He designed fish, plants and animals and they were
enamelled green, brown or yellow. All his works are considered very good because of their lifelike characters. Mr.
Poterat made a glass-like porcelain at St. Cloud in 17th
century. However, it was not until 1725 that a glassy porcelain was first produced at Chantilly. The first were copies of
Chinese and Japanese types. The King of France established
other factories very quickly in other parts of France. The
first French porcelain similar to Meissen appeared in 1769,
at the factory in Sevres. This factory is probably the most
famous in Europe. They first produced jewelled porcelain
which is the most difficult type to complete. The jewels are
turquoise, emerald, ruby, sapphire and pearls, closely made
to resemble genuine stones. The placing of these gems on the
porcelain requires the utmost skill and care.

Fine Sevres vases have brought as high as £10,000 during
the latter part of the 18th century. The most important
development in ceramic art in France occurred in 1850 when
pate-sur-pate, was developed. This is usually an enamelled
background of blue, green or red, on which a group of figures
are carved out of a white field. H. Solon is considered the
finest artist in this field of endeavor, and after leaving the
employ of the Sevres factory went to work for Mintons in
England. He was employed there for many years. Vases by
Solon are exceedingly fine and bring good prices at auction
whenever sold.

Unlike other European countries where porcelain factories were state owned or operated, or, had the co-operation
of wealthy princes and nobles, the manufacture of ceramic
art was left entirely to the individual in England. Mr.
William Cookworthy was the first Englishman to make true
porcelain and opened a factory in 1765. His wares are
known as PLYMOUTH, and are much sought after by collectors. In 1773 a Mr. Champion of Bristol, bought the
factory and patents of Mr. Cookworthy and immediately
found himself in difficulty over the patent rights. Mr.

Wedgwood was one of those who attemptd to have these patent rights cancelled. Mr. Champion was the champion, so to speak, since he won the battle. He turned out very inferior work at his factory, most of which were imitations of other factories.

England was the very first country to use ground bone which was mixed with kaolin in the manufacture of porcelain. The first style and designs were copied from Chinese and Japanese even to the marks. Japanese IMARI wares in red-gold-blue were the styles most used. German and French factories copied from English and vice-versa.

One of the most important names in porcelain is the ROYAL WORCESTER WORKS, at Worcester, England. This was established in 1751, by a Dr. Wall in company with other associates. Until the year 1770 blue and white service was made, and became the most prevailing pattern used. Nowhere in England was better porcelain produced in this color combination. It was not until 1778 when King George III and his queen visited the factory and gave permission for the use of the phrase "China Manufacturers to their Majesties" that they became really successful. Wares of this type are widely sought by collectors. The company then changed the name to the Worcester Royal Porcelain Works. Mr. Barr was taken into partnership in 1793. This period became known as the Flight and Barr period until 1807. During the Flight & Sons period the factory produced very fine pieces which were decorated so evenly and perfectly, that even though hand decorated, had the appearance of a transfer print.

In 1783 another factory was established at Worcester, then known as the Chamberlain Works. This factory usually copied other famous styles and designs, and in 1840 the two Worcester firms merged.

In 1858, when Commodore Perry opened Japan for foreign trade, this country immediately became popular and various European factories had started to imitate Japanese styles. The Worcester works were able to outclass all other factories of Europe in producing these designs. Copies of the Worcester vases were made by leading continental factories but they were never equalled. The Worcester figures and statuettes were quite outstanding and did not possess the fault of the other continental factories, whose figures all had doll-like faces. The male and female figures were exactly alike, except as to dress and hair design. In the Worcester products the figures are lifelike and different. None possess those doll-like faces, each has an expression of individuality.

Here is a short resume of some of the early English potters . . . DERBY: this factory was founded by Wm. Duesbery in 1751. He was a former decorator of china, and a man of great ambition. Shortly after starting the Derby factory he purchased the Bow works, and the Chelsea factory. He transferred their moulds and patents to his establishment at Derby. The success of this company was due to the very commercial manner in which it was operated. No new types of wares were originated, but expert imitations of other English and Continental factories were made. Robert Bloor succeeded Wm. Duesbery, son of the founder, in 1815. Later owners were Locker & Co., 1849; Stevenson & Hancock in 1859. Mr. Hancock became sole owner in 1866. In 1877 E. Phillips, Mr. Litherland and J. McInness started operations as "Crown Derby Porcelain Co." and in 1891 the term "Royal" was granted. Articles made by the Derby works are of exquisite whiteness and decorated very tastefully and beautifully. Innumerable articles such as vases, service and figures were made here during the 19th century. The decorations were of floral designs, and often gilt floral sprays were used.

Designs of birds and insects were also occasionally used. The later owners were highly jealous of their wares and employed high-priced workmen to decorate their china, and never permitted inferior pieces to leave their factory. Early in the 19th century some poorer pieces were sold and this caused a temporary decline in their reputations.

The Doulton works are a comparatively new factory, having been established in 1872 by Mr. Henry Doulton. This is now one of the most important in England. Mr. Doulton was famous for his experiments in enamelling. His wares are known for their fine enamels, etched designs and the great variety of vases, figures and service. The flower work on the vases is soft and well executed. Among their early pieces, which were always decorated by the finest artists available, are the best collectors' items of today.

DAVENPORT — This company was founded by John Davenport, who is known for the exceptionally fine china and earthenware which was turned out at his factory. Good artists were used for the decorations. The theme of these decorations were usually birds and flowers. This firm is also famous for their fine china service, which usually had a yellow or blue border with a floral decoration in the center. This company, unfortunately, has ceased operations.

COPELAND—was founded by Josiah Spode, in 1770. His son Josiah, Jr., succeeded him. This firm was among the first English factories that used bone in the manufacture of porcelain. Under the management of Josiah, Jr., the firm became quite famous, but was purchased in 1833 by Mr. Copeland and became known as Copeland China. The son of Mr. Copeland, who was connected with his father in this purchase, helped produce a ware known as opaque porcelain, which was very durable. This factory is one of the foremost in England, and are also noted for their decorations, which are quite brilliant.

BOW—was established in 1740. Nothing was heard about these products until 1744 when they commenced to manufacture a soft-paste porcelain. Ground bone was also later used in this product. This firm was among those later purchased by Mr. Duesbery of Derby, who removed the patents and moulds to Derby. They had made great varieties of vases, figures of animals, birds and groups of statuettes. The quality of work from this factory was very irregular and in many cases very poor. It may interest you to know that clay from America was used in the making of this ware. No factory marks were used on the Bow products but bows, arrows, daggers and anchors were impressed and marked. There is considerable doubt as to the authenticity of some of these marks.

CHELSEA—The Duke of Cumberland and Sir Everhard Fowkener started this work in 1745. Mr. N. Sprimont purchased it in 1775 and ran it until he sold it to Mr. Duesbery of the Derby Works the same year. However Mr. Duesbery ran it as an individual factory until 1784, when he removed the moulds to Derby. They had produced many beautiful and artistic creations at this factory. They had become. famous for their flower decorations in relief. They also made candelabra, vases, figures, groups and service. The statuettes were usually patriotic figures of that time. Figures of Grecian and Roman characters were also produced. The mark was an anchor of different shapes. These are now widely imitated for a great deal of so-called Chelsea with anchor marks are seen, but actually the factory ceased to exist in 1784.

COALPORT—The Caughley factory was purchased by John Rose in 1799. This factory had been located in Colebrook-Dale. He removed this factory to Coalport in 1814, later in 1820 the Swansea and Nantgarrow factories were added to this combine. Mr. Billingsley, a famous decorator, was employed here to decorate these porcelain wares. Most of these decorations were flowers and birds. The works of this artist are much sought after. This factory for a long period of time copied other factories wares and styles, even to the marks. Excellent copies of the Dresden, Meissen, Sevres and Chelsea were produced here. Towards the latter part of the 19th century they began to make finely jewelled porcelain, and beautiful enamelled vases, tea and coffee service. Many examples of these appeared in international exhibitions held all over the world. These pieces are very highly prized by collectors, both amateur and professional.

MINTONS—This factory was established in 1790 by Mr. Thomas Minton, and is still among the best today. It is now known as Mintons China. In 1798 Mr. Minton introduced a semi-transparent china, which was finally perfected by this company in 1821. This firm sent many styles and decorations of service to America during the 19th century. The most famous porcelain product from Mintons was known as Pate-sur-pate, which the Sevres factories originated. The Minton factory hired Mr. Solon, a former employee of Sevres, who improved on the original pate-sur-pate. The pieces made by Solon are very famous.

COBRIDGE—Started operations in a factory owned by Ralph Daniel. John Warburton later became head of this firm and was succeeded by his wife after his death. Mrs.

Warburton was known as an excellent decorator, was famous for her enamelling. Josiah Wedgwood sent many undecorated pieces to her, for decorations and enamelling.

J. and R. Clews were potters in Cobridge as well, and were well-known for their early American scenes and portraits which decorated their china. One of their most famous designs is the elaborate one showing the Landing of Lafayette at Castle Garden. In 1836, Clews established a factory of his own in Troy, Indiana.

A Frenchman, formerly employed by Wedgwood, opened a factory here in 1770. His name was J. Voyez, his work was producing pieces similar to Wedgwood. His copies of Wedgwood cameos, intaglios and other Wedgwood ornaments were exceptionally fine. On some he placed the Wedgwood mark. While most of these pieces are well made they are considered inferior to the originals.

BROWNFIELD—Brownfield, Wood and Robinson opened a factory at Cobridge in 1836. They were succeeded in 1850 by W. Brownfield & Sons. They are principally known for their service, which was produced in large quantities.

BOOTH'S CHINA—This firm started operations in 1870 and is still in existence. Famous also for their many qualities of service, which were usually designed with floral backgrounds.

WEDGWOOD—Most every schoolboy knows of Wedgwood, since there are many books written about the founder of this firm. Josiah Wedgwood was born in 1730, youngest of thirteen children. In 1752, together with John Harrison, he entered into a partnership to manufacture pottery. They soon broke this partnership and young Josiah returned to Burslem, where he secured work as an apprentice. In 1768, with Thomas Bentley as his new partner, he started to manufacture a ware known as ETRURIA. Bentley died in 1780, and Wedgwood's three sons were taken into partnership. Josiah died in 1795. Since that time the eldest son of the eldest son has continued to head this vast enterprise. Josiah, Senior, who started with little or no education succeeded in leaving behind him a reputation in ceramic art that is second to none. Most of us are familiar with the most famous of the Wedgwood pieces. He called this Jasper

Ware. It took him ten years to perfect this terra cotta, and finally in 1774 he started making vases, cameos, intaglios in this type of ware, which became the game of many copyists. In 1762 Wedgwood made a complete service for the queen, and this became known as Queensware. Later he made a service for the King of England. This ware was known as the Royal Pattern. He became quite famous because of this, so that orders flowed in steady streams from that point onward. This firm, still in existence today, manufactures vases, figures and service, and also the well-known Jasper Ware. They are also famous for making the first copy of the famed "Portland Vase," which had been broken by a fanatic, and repaired by Josiah Wedgwood.

BROWN WESTHEAD & MOORE & CO.—They became known as the Cauldon China Works. This was established in 1794 by Job Rigway. John and William Rigway were the ones who succeeded Job. In 1860, Mr. Brown Westhead and Mr. Moore took over the business. This firm produced blue and white service, mostly for American consumption. On the many plates made by this firm, duplication of scenes were effected, so that the State House at Boston, and the City Hall of New York are exactly alike. Both views, however, are of City Hall in New York. Later, they made a great variety of pieces which were extremely lifelike, with raised leaves, flowers and birds. These usually have a fine white background, and two or three colors of gold decorations are used. This style of decoration was later copied by other English manufacturers.

LOWESTOFT—Walker & Brown & Co. started operations in a factory at Lowestoft about the middle of the 18th century. They manufactured pottery and soft-paste porcelain. First pieces were decorated in blue, some with scenes of nearby views. Chinese designs were also copied at this time. In 1775 this firm began to make true porcelain, which at first had ordinary patterns. Later Chinese motifs were introduced, and made in such great quantities that many dealers believe that they were made in China and sent to England to be sold as English merchandise. There is no positive basis for these claims. Later, the decorations had sprays of flowers and small animals. A great many of the Lowestoft products were exported to the United States. Many Americans believed that their ancestors had bought these pieces in China, because of the Chinese decorations and marks, which included crests, seals and initials. The Chinese porcelain is better and whiter, and should not be hard to distinguish from the Lowestoft pieces. Today the Chinese make excellent copies of this ware, which is itself a copy of Chinese originally. It may be interesting to know that the Lowestoft factory never marked their products and eventually went out of business in 1804.

BELEEK—This is the only Irish porcelain firm of great renown. They specialize in the making of a very fine and thin eggshell type of service. This style of shell work is used almost exclusively. This finished product is unusually delicate. This firm also used an iridescent lustre to finish their wares. There are a number of American Beleek factories established in Trenton, New Jersey, who manufacture a similar type of porcelain. Although the work is equally good, the American product does not have the thin effect of the Irish ware.

During the early 19th century many English, and other continental workmen migrated to this country and started factories of their own. Most factories were established in the East, especially in Trenton, New Jersey, and Ohio, since these scenes were close to the clay territory. After a few years most of these factories went out of business. Among the better known early American factories was the one at Burlington, Vermont. They were famous for a type of brownish looking pottery. This was a heavy sort of ware, with figures, animals, pitchers and service.

The most famous of all American factories is the Lenox factory at Trenton. This company produces wares such as service, vases, figures and other ornaments. During the 19th century many beautiful copies of continental porcelain was produced here. It specialized in copies of Beleek and also used a lotus leaf pattern exclusively. The Willets China of Trenton also made exceptionally fine porcelain in the Beleek style.

Another well-known American factory was established by a Mrs. Storer late in the 19th century, in Cincinnati, Ohio.

These products are known as the Rockwood Pottery, with a style of decoration that is usually a dark brown background, highly glazed, with colored leaves and flowers heavily raised, and exceptionally well painted.

————————————————

PARTIAL LIST OF PRICES PREVAILING
DURING THE 19th CENTURY

PRICES OF SÈVRES: BERNAL SALE, 1855.

In March, 1855, the collection of works of art of the late Ralph Bernal, Esq., including a large amount of pottery and porcelain, was sold at auction in London. The prices obtained for Sèvres wares were supposed to mark the highest limit which they would be likely to attain, and the prices of fine specimens of such kinds as are more commonly met with have not materially advanced; while *vieux Sèvres* vases of fine character have since that date advanced enormously.

			£	s.	d.
Cup and saucer, blue-ribbon border, roses in compartments			5	5	0
"	"	apple-green, exotic birds in compartments	7	17	6
"	"	gros bleu, with Cupids	17	17	0
"	"	green, Venus chastising Cupid, and a dog, in landscape	26	0	0
"	"	two children, etc., painted by Leguay	22	1	0
"	"	green, figures, etc., painted by Chabry and Merault	55	0	0
"	"	gros bleu and green, with Cupids	18	11	6
"	"	gros bleu and green, children, painted by Viellard	27	6	0
"	"	turquoise, exotic birds	9	9	0
"	"	gros bleu, figures in landscape, painted by Chabry	32	11	0
"	"	gros bleu, nymph reposing, painted by Chabry	6	6	0
"	"	Rose Du Barri, landscapes, 1757	22	0	0
"	"	white, Cupids in blue, painted by Dodet, 1763	19	19	0
"	"	gros bleu, exotic birds	4	4	0

PRICES AT SALE OF THE COLLECTION OF A. MORSE, ESQ., LONDON, MARCH, 1876.

	£	s.	d.
Bow :			
Figure of Winter	5	7	6
Two dogs in an arbor	2	10	0
Milk-jug, form of two goats, bee in relief	3	5	0
Figure of Neptune, 9 inches high	8	15	0
Butter-boat	0	13	0
Bristol :			
Pair of butter-boats, embossed and painted with flowers	4	15	0
Mug, flowers and insects	6	0	0
Pair of figures, shepherd and milkmaid	126	0	0
Chelsea :			
Pair of pastoral figures	12	15	0
Figure, Romeo, 12½ inches high	27	0	0
" Milton, 12 inches high	8	10	0
Pair of figures, pedlers	52	0	0
Teapot, flowers	1	5	0
Coffee-pot, flowers	3	15	0
Cup and saucer, gold and flowers	3	9	0
Plate, flowers	2	0	0
Fruit-dish, fruit, flowers, insects	3	15	0
Figure, girl by urn, 8½ inches high	6	0	0
Vase, florid rococo style, raised flowers, medallions of Cupids	25	4	0
Chelsea Derby :			
Four figures, Europe, Asia, Africa, America, 13 inches high	74	11	0
Derby :			
Plate, medallion of hunting subject	2	4	0
Cream-ewer, helmet shape, gold and blue	0	15	0
Vase, 13 inches high, landscapes	11	0	0
Vase, medallion, birds	2	0	0
Cup and saucer, flowers	0	9	0
Pair of vases, mask handles, bird	3	3	0
Plymouth :			
Pair of groups, Cupids and goats, 8 inches high	28	7	0
Open-work basket, white, with raised flowers	4	0	0
Salt-stands, pair, encrusted with shells	6	16	0
" " rustic groups, foliage, etc.	42	0	0
Swansea :			
Cup and saucer, flowers	2	0	0
Plate, large bouquet	5	5	0
Pair of plates, fruit, flowers, birds	2	15	0
Worcester :			
Mug, parrots and fruit	0	15	0
Two cream-jugs, Chinese figures, etc.	0	7	0
Pair of coffee-cups, print, garden party	2	15	0
Cup and saucer, flowers in blue	1	5	0
" " turquoise borders, flowers	3	12	0
" " green border, flowers	1	5	0

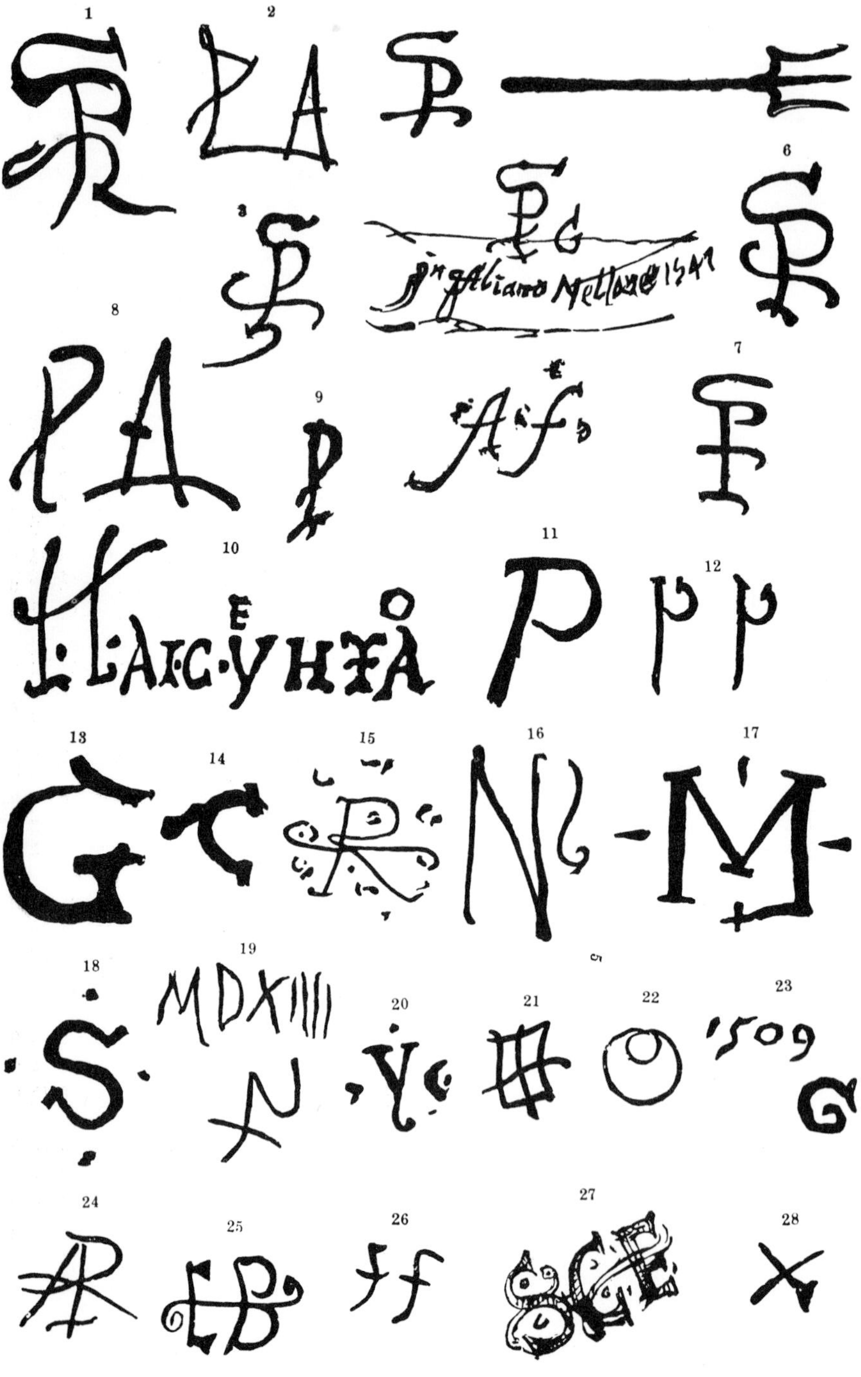
MDXIIII
1509

1-28. CAFFAGIUOLO. Early Italian pottery marks. The forms of these marks vary greatly. Often the individual artists used their own names and initials as marks. These were also impressed on their works. Some specimens are attributed to the 15th century, although most of the pieces found can be attributed after 1507.

An unusual fine white background with a brilliant red, or vivid rich dark blue, are the most frequently used decorations. Of course other colors were used, but none as distinctive as the blue and red.

29. SIENA. Early Italian pottery resembling CAFFAGIUOLO.

30. PISA. Specimens of PISA works are known to have existed as early as the 13th century. A vase with serpent handles, with the mark of PISA, is probably the best known example.

31. UNKNOWN MARK.

32-34. MONTE-LUPO. Dark colored brown or black pottery was made here. This was usually gilded at the border, and oil paintings in various colors used to decorate the wares.

35-49. GUBBIO. The work of Gubbio is centered on the artist GIORGIO ANDREOLI, who came to Gubbio late in the 15th century, and is well known for the brilliant gem-like coloring which he produced. Best known are the red and blue lustres. Master Andreoli also produced work in raised relief.

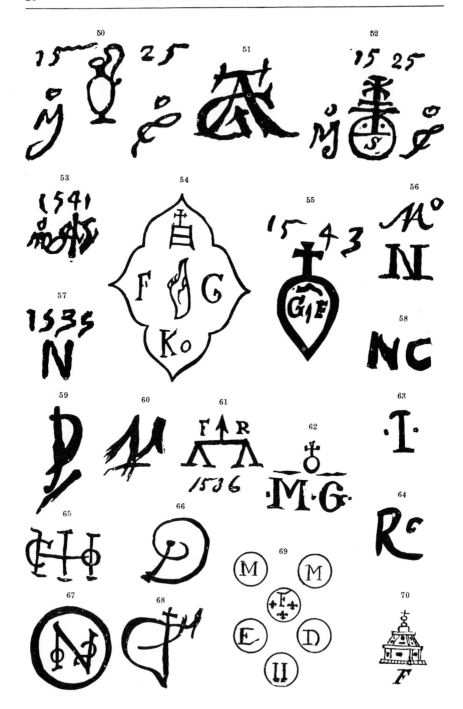

50-68. GUBBIO.

69-70. MEDICI. FRANCESCO de MEDICI first produced artificial porcelain, not unlike that of the Chinese in 1575, at FLORENCE, and of course it was a sort of copy of Chinese work of that period.

71-76. CASTEL-DURANTE. What was perhaps the largest pottery-producing factory of Europe in the 14th to 16th centuries, was located here, and its ware were sold all over Europe. These wares were usually decorated with monsters, dragons, and other medieval animals.

77-100. URBINO. What was probably the best known pottery up to the 18th century was established here by the Duke of Urbino, late 16th century. The best known German, Italian, French and other good artists were employed here to decorate the wares, plates, figures, vases, and other pottery forms produced.

101-107. DIRUTA. Early 16th century.

108. FABRIANO. Early 16th century.

109-111. ROME. This factory commenced operation early 18th century, and continued until closed late in the 18th century. Vases, figures, service and other pottery products were made here, and during the final period of its operation, produced copies of Wedgewood's QUEENSWARE.

112-122. FAENZA. Pottery products were made here during the 15th to 18th centuries. These were usually copies of other factories of that period. The products made here were considered as good as pieces produced elsewhere.

123-142. FAENZA.

143-145. FORLI. Master JERONIMO had a factory here during the very late 15th and early 16th centuries. He made excellent majolica type wares.

146. RAVENNA.

147-148. RIMINI. All known pieces of RIMINI are dated 1535.

149

150

151

152

153
Antonia Teruf;
in
Bassano

154
Bᵒ Terchj
Bassano.

155

156

157
1564

158

159

160

161
B C

162
A
G. G.
F

163

164
S

165

166

167

168
Jean·gony

169

170
Milano
F 4/Ω C

171
Milano F±/Ω C

172
P. R.
Milᵒ

173
M^le Brecchi

174
M
Lodi 1764

175

176
·N·

177
Nᵘᵉ O:
G·B·A·B:

178
S.I.G
1750

179
1723

149. VENICE.

150. CORNARO.

151. TREVISO.

152-154. BASSANO.

155. VERONA. 14th, 15th and 16th century Italian potters.

156-157. PADUA.

158. GENOA.

159. GENOA.

160-164. SAVONA.

165-167. TURIN.

168. MAURIENNE.

169-173. MILAN.

174-175. LODI.

176. TREVISO.

177-178. NOVE. During the 18th century this place became the best known Italian pottery-producing centre. In 1728 G. B. Antonibon produced some fine pieces and offered them for sale in Venice, and later produced wares with great care and skill. There is a record of their works until late 19th century.

179. PESARO.

180-186. NAPLES. Factories are known to have existed here during the 16th century. Little of important works were produced here. The last two marks (185-6) are of 18th century potters.

187. PESARO. 15th and 16th century.

188-190. Established by the GIUSTINI BROTHERS, at Naples, late 18th century. Fine works were produced here, especially copies of the English QUEENSWARE, which was very popular in Italy during this time.

191-193. CASTELLI. 16th and 17th century. During the late 17th century this factory outranked all others in Italy for the fine wares it produced. Also at Castelli, a family of decorators known as GRUE, became very famous for their works. This was during the 18th century, and to this family the CAPO-di-MONTE factory owes its existence, for they trained many of the artists employed here.

194-198. Marquis Ginori founded a factory at La Doccia, near Florence in 1737, and has since remained in the same family control. Italian porcelain was first produced here, and great importance was stressed on the character of their products. Vases, figures, service, and other wares were made. The finest and most skilled artists of Europe were employed here. This factory at a later date obtained the Capo-di-Monte moulds, and has since produced this type of wares. The factory is the largest and most famous in Italy today, and enjoys worldwide reputation.

199-205. CAPO-di-MONTE. This factory was first established by Charles 3rd, at Naples, 1736. Charles took great pride in this factory, and was often seen working here. The factory continued to operate until closed in 1821. Ferdinand 4th, in 1759, obtained some of the Capo-di-Monte workmen, sent them to Madrid, and established a factory known as the BUEN RETIRO. Fine specimens of the Capo-di-Monte works are now getting rare. Enormous quantities were first produced for Italian consumption, but owing to the fame of this factory in recent years they are very scarce now. When the Ginori factory obtained the moulds when this factory closed, they also retained the mark, and are still using this mark, making the same objects, although fine specimens, especially those with colored relief, are costly. The pieces made at the Ginori factory are usually more brilliant and gaudy, the porcelain heavier, and the color more milky. Many Dresden and French factories also make imitations of the Capo-di-Monte articles.

FRENCH POTTERY MARKS

1. BEAUVAIS. Perhaps as far as the 14th century, pottery was first made here. RABELAIS has a passage in which he speaks of a "goubelet de Beavoys." Many doubtful specimens of this early ware exist.

2. OIRON. Italy and Germany during the 14th, 15th and 16th centuries were making rapid strides in the manufacture of pottery. France during this time was content to import these products, and did little or nothing during this period to manufacture any of its own pottery products. It was content to use their own poor and unimportant pieces for use and decorations. A lady of wealth, a Mrs. Helen de Hangest-Genlis, widow of Arthur Gouffier, became the godmother of pottery of France. She lived at Oiron and employed a Jean Bernart and Francois Carpentier, and these two made some good articles of pottery.

3. AVON. Factory was in existence here in 1608; figures, statuettes and animals were made here.

4-66. ROUEN. The potteries of Rouen are considered the most important of early French factories. M. BAQUESNE made fine enamelled pottery of great beauty during the years 1535 to 1557, and his widow and son continued after his demise. Later many others opened factories at Rouen and continued to operate successfully. Louis Poterat obtained in 1673 a grant to make porcelain similar to the Chinese. Although the French claim that Poterat was the first to make soft paste porcelain, it is not supported. He did, however, make fine copies of Chinese wares, but this was a glasslike porcelain. 65-66 are the marks of A. POTERAT.

These factories were established during the 17th and 18th centuries, first made pottery, and later soft and hard-paste porcelains. Most of these were later absorbed into the Sevres Works.

67-75. LILLE.

76. VALENCIENNES.

77-81. ST. AMAND LES EAUX.

82-84. PARIS.

85-87. SCEAUX.

88. BOURG LA REINE.

89. ST. CLOUD.

90-92. SINCENY.

93-98. APREY.

99. MATHAULT.

100-105a. NIDERVILLER.

106. SARREGUEMINES.

107-114. STRASSBOURG.

115. PREMIERES.

116. MEILLONAS.

117-118. VARGAS.

119-121. TAVERNE.

122-152. MOUSTIERS.

153. MENNECY.

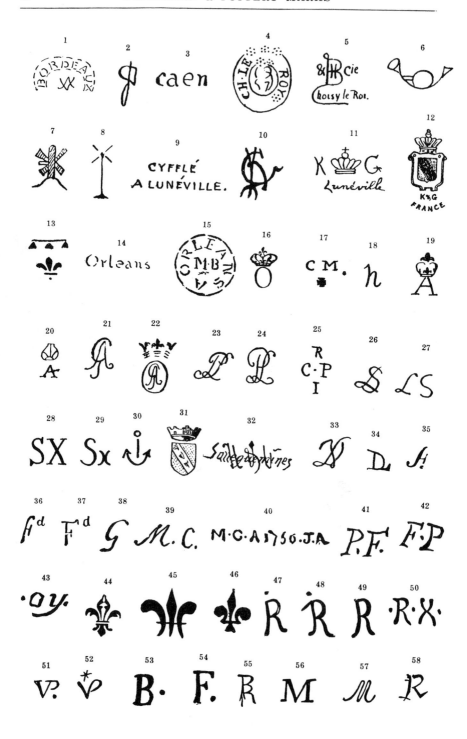

1-6. ARRAS. Established in 1784, and after four or five years of operation went out of business. Their work often equalled the Sevres, which it imitated. Sometimes these articles are disfigured with small particles of coal due to a faulty kiln.

7-8. CLIGANCOURT. Factory opened 1775 by Pierre Deruelle, under the patronage of the Count de Provence. Products produced here are known as PORCELAINE DE MONSIEUR.

9-12. LUNEVILLE. Also known as (KELLER & GUERIN). In 1778 Keller & Guerrin purchased a factory here and produced soft-paste, in such forms as animals used as door-stops. Later this company continued to manufacture a fine variety of porcelain products.

13-16. Established 1784 by the Duke of Orleans.

17-25. PARIS. Many individual factories were established during the 18th century. Often well-known decorators' names appear on these products, who formerly worked in the smaller shops, until absorbed by the Sevres works.

26-30. SCEAUX. Established by Jaques Chapelle, 1750, for the manufacture of soft paste, and continued until the close of the century.

31-32. SARREGUEMINES. Established 1770, by PAUL UTZ-SCHNEIDER, these are 19th century marks. This factory enjoys worldwide reputation, and much of its products are sent to America.

33-34. VALENCIENNES. Established 1785, made bisque figures.

35-43. MOUSTIERS. Several potteries to manufacture hard and soft paste porcelains were established here during the 18th century.

44-54. MARSEILLES. Madame Savy, widow of Perrin, established a factory here, also Mr. Robert was supposed to make true porcelain products here.

55-57. MARANS. Established 1740, made products similar to Rouen, owner Jean Pierre Roussencq.

58. RENAC. Established about 1762. Made articles similar to RENNES.

59-70. NEVERS. Early French potters, established by Dominique Conrade, Italian with two brothers, in 1578, only potters here until 1632, when B. Bourcier founded another. In the 18th century many others were added. The first products were copies of Italian wares, later original products of their own individual style were made. Soft- and hard-paste porcelain was made here during the 18th century.

71. LIMOGES. Established in 1774 by M. Massie, made soft paste, later other works were established, and others suspended. Also in 1774 a factory making hard-paste porcelain was established here, and still continues to operate. The first owner was M. ALLUAUD. Many other factories have been established here during the 19th century.

72. LA TOUR D'AIGUES. Established 1782.

73. AVISSEAU.

74-93. Undetermined marks of French factories.

93-112. Undetermined marks found on French porcelains.

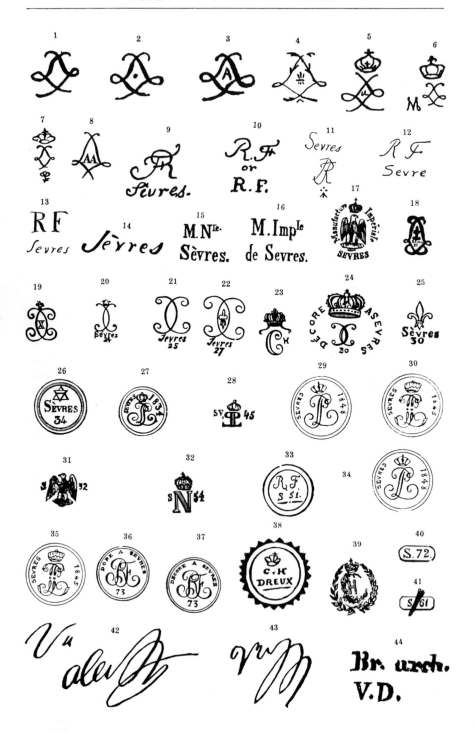

SEVRES

1-4. VINCENNES, at St. Cloud, was considered by many Frenchmen to have first made porcelain, and in 1740, two brothers named DUBOIS, ex-workmen at St. Cloud, offered to sell to M. Orry de Fulvy, the secret of making porcelain. A factory at Vincennes was started, and after 3 years of unsuccessful efforts at porcelain making they were discharged. The works continued, and in 1745 Charles Adam was given permission by the French King, Louis XV, to continue operations for 30 years. The first products of the factory at Vincennes seem to have been articles imitating oriental wares. Madame Pompadour was said to have taken great interest in this first great French porcelain factory. So great was the demand for these products, that in 1756 the works were removed to a special factory erected for them at Sevres, and Louis XV became the sole owner, and a decree issued in 1760 provided that its new name would be MANUFAC-TURE DE PORCELAINE DE FRANCE. This name was later dropped, and the name Sevres used. So great was the reputation of this factory that another decree was issued forbidding other factories from copying or gilding any of their wares to resemble articles produced at Sevres. Hard-paste porcelain was made. Articles of great beauty were produced. Here also the first jewelled porcelain was made. In 1780 colored paste resembling the ruby, pearl, sapphire and emerald were applied as decorations on their wares. Statuettes, animals and service were made. The most famous service made here was one made for the Empress Catherine 2nd of Russia, in 1778. This consisted of 744 pieces, and costing at that time over $200,000. Some 160 of these were later stolen at a fire at the palace, and found their way in England. A few pieces still remain in private collections. A plate of this service was sold at auction in February, 1875, and brought $1500.00. A tremendous amount of "phoney" Sevres exists. This mark is probably forged more often than any others.

5-7. Became known as Sevres works, and the crown was added.

8. Sevres mark of 1777, the first of the double letters used to denote date.

9-13. First marks of Republican period, 1792 to 1800.

14. Word Sevres alone used.

15. Mark of 1803.

16-17. 1804 to 1814.

18. Mark of Louis XVIII, 1814 to 1824.

19-22. Mark of Charles X, 1824 to 1828.

23-30. Mark of Louis-Phillipe, 1830 to 1848.

31-37. Mark of the Empire under Napoleon.

38. Mark placed on pieces intended for royalty.

39. Mark on pieces made for Catherine 2nd of Russia.

40-41. Mark adopted 1848, letter "S" plus the last two ciphers are for the date of the year in which the article was made. Thus S.72 in 1872, and etc.

42-44. Marks of individual Sevres artists placed on pieces made by them, early 19th century.

1-18. Unknown French Pottery marks.

1-30.. Various marks used by LIMOGE manufacturers, 1842 to 1898. These factories enjoyed worldwide reputations. Although they made every type of porcelain product, their reputations are chiefly founded on their service, in which they probably excel. Many American importers of porcelain had their own trade-mark placed on these wares.

MARKS USED BY PAINTERS, DECORATORS, AND GILDERS AT SÈVRES.

FIRST PERIOD. 1753–1799.

Aloncle—birds, animals, emblems, etc.

Anteaume—landscape, animals.

Armand—birds, flowers, etc.

Asselin—portraits, miniatures, etc.

Aubert (senior)—flowers.

Bailly (son)—flowers.

Bardet—flowers.

Barre—detached bouquets.

Barrat—garlands, bouquets.

Baudoin—ornaments, friezes, etc.

Becquet—flowers, etc.

Bertrand—detached bouquets.

Bienfait—gilding.

Binet—detached bouquets.

Binet, Madame (née *Sophie Chanou*)—flowers.

Boucher—flowers, garlands, etc.

Bouchet—landscape, figures, ornaments.

Bouillat—flowers, landscapes.

Boulanger—detached bouquets.

Boulanger (son)—pastoral subjects, children.

Bulidon—detached bouquets.

Bunel, Madame (née *Manon Buteux*)—flowers.

Bunel, Madame—another form.

Buteux (senior)—flowers, emblems, etc.

Buteux (elder son)—detached bouquets, etc.

Buteux (younger son)—pastoral subjects, children.

Capel—friezes.

Cardin—detached bouquets.

Carrier—flowers.

Castel—landscapes, hunts, birds.

Caton—pastoral subjects, children, birds.

Catrice—flowers, detached bouquets.

Chabry—miniatures, pastoral subjects.

Chanou, Madame (née *Julie Durosey*)—flowers.

Chapuis (elder)—flowers, birds, etc.

Chapuis (younger)—detached bouquets.

Chauvaux (father)—gilding.

Chauvaux (son)—detached bouquets, gilding.

Chevalier—flowers, bouquets, etc.

Choisy, De—flowers, arabesques.

Chulot—emblems, flowers, arabesques.

Commelin—detached bouquets, garlands.

Cornaille—flowers, detached bouquets.

Couturier—gilding.	
Dieu—Chinese, Chinese flowers, gilding, etc.	
Dodin—figure, various subjects, portraits.	
Drand—Chinese, gilding.	
Dubois—flowers, garlands, etc.	
Dusolle—detached bouquets, etc.	
Dutanda—detached bouquets, garlands.	
Evans—birds, butterflies, landscapes.	
Falot—arabesques, birds, butterflies.	
Fontaine—emblems, miniatures, etc.	
Fontelliau—gilding, etc.	
Fouré—flowers, bouquets, etc.	
Fritsch—figures, children.	
Fumez—detached bouquets.	
Fumez—another form.	
Gauthier—landscape and animals.	
Genest—figure and genre.	
Genin—flowers, garlands, friezes, etc.	
Gerard—pastoral subjects, miniatures.	
Gerard, Madame (née *Vautrin*)—flowers.	
Girard—arabesques, Chinese, etc.	
Gomery—flowers and birds.	
Gremont—garlands, bouquets.	
Grison—gilding.	

Henrion—garlands, detached bouquets.

Héricourt—garlands, detached bouquets.

Hilken—figures, pastoral subjects, etc.

Houry—flowers, etc.

Huny—flowers, detached bouquets.

Joyau—detached bouquets, etc.

Jubin—gilding.

La Roche—flowers, garlands, emblems.

La Roche—another form.

Le Bel (elder)—figures and flowers.

Le Bel (younger)—garlands, bouquets, etc.

Léandre—pastoral subjects, miniatures.

Lecot—Chinese, etc.

Lecot—another form.

Ledoux—landscape and birds.

Le Guay—gilding.

Le Guay—another form.

Leguay—miniatures, children, Chinese.

Levé (father)—flowers, birds, arabesques.

Levé, Félix—flowers, Chinese.

Maqueret, Madame (née *Bouillat*)—flowers.

Massy—groups of flowers, garlands.

Merault (elder)—friezes.

Merault (younger)—bouquets, garlands.

Micaud—flowers, bouquets, medallions.

Michel—detached bouquets.

Moiron—detached bouquets; also another form used by *Michel.*

Mongenot — flowers, detached bouquets.

Morin—marine, military subjects.

Mutel—landscape.

Niquet—detached bouquets, etc.

Noel—flowers, ornaments.

Nouailhier, Madame (née Sophie Durosy)—flowers.

Parpette — flowers, detached bouquets.

Parpette, Dlle. Louison—flowers.

Pajou—figure.

Petit—flowers.

Pfeiffer—detached bouquets.

Pierre (elder)—flowers, bouquets.

Pierre (younger) — bouquets, garlands.

Philippine (elder) — pastoral subjects, children, etc.

Pithou (elder)—portraits, historical subjects.

Pithou (younger)—figures, flowers, ornaments.

Pouillot—detached bouquets.

Prevost—gilding.

Raux—detached bouquets.

Rochet—figure, miniatures, etc.

Rosset—landscape, etc.

Roussel—detached bouquets.

Schradre—birds, landscape, etc.

Sinsson—flowers, groups, garlands, etc.

Sioux (elder)—detached bouquets, garlands.

Sioux (younger)—flowers, garlands.

Tabary—birds, etc.

Taillandier — detached bouquets, garlands.

Tandart — groups of flowers, garlands.

Tardi—detached bouquets, etc.

Theodore—gilding.

Thevenet (father)—flowers, medallions, groups, etc.

Thevenet (son)—ornaments, friezes, etc.

Vandé—gilding, flowers.

Vavasseur—arabesques.

Vieillard—emblems, ornaments, etc.

Vincent—gilding.

Xrowet—arabesques, flowers, etc.

Yvernel—landscape, birds.

SECOND PERIOD.   1800–1874.

André, Jules—landscape.

Apoil—figures, subjects, etc.

Apoil, Madame—figure.

Archelais—ornament worker (pâtes sur pâtes).

Avisse—ornament worker.

Barbin—ornaments.

Ⱥ	*Barré*—flowers.
ᗷ.	*Barriat*—figure.
ℬ.ᵣ	*Beranger*—figure.
B	*Blanchard*—decorator.
ₐℬ	*Blanchard, Alex.*—ornament worker.
ℬ.ᒃ	*Boitel*—gilding.
ₐℬ	*Bonnuit*—decorator.
Ⱥ	*Boullemier, Antoine*—gilding.
ℱ.ℬ	*Boullemier* (elder)—gilding.
ℬf	*Boullemier* (son)—gilding.
ℬᵪ.	*Buteux*—flowers.
CC	*Cabau*—flowers.
Cℙ	*Capronnier*—gilding.
ℐC	*Célos*—ornament worker (pâtes sur pates).
LC	*Charpentier*—decorator.
ℱ.C.	*Charrin, Dlle. Fanny*—figures, subjects, portraits.
C.C.	*Constant*—gilding.
C.ᒃ.	*Constantin*—figure.
ₐⅅ	*Dammouse*—figure, ornament (pâtes sur pâtes).
ⅅ	*David*—decorator.
ⅅ.ℱ.	*Delafosse*—figure.
ⅅ.ℱ	*Davignon*—landscape.
ⅅ.ℒ.	*Desperais*—ornaments.
ⅅC	*Derichsweiller*—decorator.
CD	*Develly*—landscape and genre.
ⅅₕ	*Deutsch*—ornaments.
ⅅ.Í.	*Didier*—ornaments, etc.
ⅅ:	*Didier*—another form.
ⅅ.ᒃ	*Drouet*—flowers.
ₐⅅ	*Ducluzeau, Madame* — figure, subjects, portraits, etc.
ⅅᵧ	*Durosey*—gilding.
HF	*Farraguet, Madame* — figure, subjects, etc.
ℱC	*Ficquenet*—flowers and ornaments (pâtes sur pâtes).
ℱ	*Fontaine*—flowers.
ᒃℬ	*Fragonard*—figure, genre, etc.
Cᵤ	*Ganeau* (son)—gilding.
Ɪ.C	*Gély*—ornament worker (pâtes sur pâtes).
ℊ.ℊ.	*Georget*—figure, portraits, etc.
Cₒᵦ.ℛ	*Gobert*—figure on enamel and on pastes.
ⅅ.ℊ.	*Godin*—*gilding*.
ℱ.ℊ.	*Goupil*—figure.
ℂⅅ	*Guillemain*—decorator.
H	*Hallion, Eugène*—landscape.
H	*Hallion, François*—decorator in gilding.
ₕ.�Ĵ.	*Huard*—ornaments, divers styles.
.C.ᕼ.	*Humbert*—figure.
É	*Julienne* — ornaments, style Renaissance, etc.
ℋ	*Lambert*—flowers.
ℒ ℊᵘ	*Langlacé*—landscape.
Ɪ	*Latache*—gilding.
ℒ.ℬ.	*Le Bel*—landscape.
ℒ	*Legay*—ornament worker (pâtes sur pâtes).
ℓ.ℊ.	*Le Gay*—figures, various subjects, portraits.
ℓℊ	*Legrand*—gilding.
ℰL	*Leroy, Eugène*—gilding.

Martinet—flowers.	
Maussion, Mdlle. de—figure.	
Merigot—ornaments, etc.	
Meyer, Alfred—figure, etc.	
Micaud—gilding.	
Milet, Optat—decorator on faience and pastes.	
Moreau—gilding.	
Moriot—figure, etc.	
Parpette, Dlle.—flowers.	
Philippine—flowers and ornaments.	
Pline—decorative gilding.	
Poupart—landscape.	
Regnier, Ferd.—figure, various subjects.	
Regnier, Hyacinthe—figure.	
Rejoux—decorator.	
Renard, Émile—decorator.	
Richard, Émile—flowers.	
Richard, Eugène—flowers.	

Richard, François—decorator.

Richard, Joseph—decorator.

Richard, Paul—decorative gilding.

Riocreux, Isidore—landscape.

Riocreux, Désiré-Denis—flowers.

Robert, Pierre—landscape.

Robert, Madame—flowers and landscape.

Robert, Jean-François—landscape.

Roussel—figure, etc.

Schilt, Louis-Pierre—flowers.

Sinsson (father)—flowers.

Solon—figures and ornaments (pâtes sur pâtes).

Swebach—landscape and genre.

Trager—flowers, birds.

Troyon—ornaments.

Walter—flowers.

UNDETERMINED SIGNATURES, ETC.

Three marks on plate dated 1821, view of Moka, signed L. M., richly gilded. The first mark also on several plates dated 1812, lapis-lazuli borders, heavy gilding, antique cameo paintings.

Marks used at Sevres to denote year of manufacture.

A	1753	I	1761	Q	1769
B	1754	J	1762	R	1770
C	1755	K	1763	S	1771
D	1756	L	1764	T	1772
E	1757	M	1765	U	1773
F	1758	N	1766	W	1774
G	1759	O	1767	X	1775
H	1760	P	1768	Y	1776
				Z	1777

Some authorities believe that the letter "J" was never used and the letter "K" was used for 1762 instead, the letter "L" used for 1763 and etc.

AA	1778	GG	1784	MM	1790
BB	1779	HH	1785	NN	1791
CC	1780	II	1786	OO	1792
DD	1781	JJ	1787	PP	1793
EE	1782	KK	1788	QQ	1794
FF	1783	LL	1789	RR	1795

After 1795 the double lettering was not used, with rare exceptions.

In 1818 the practice of using the last two numerals of the year was adopted, so that in 1818 the number "18" was used, and so on.

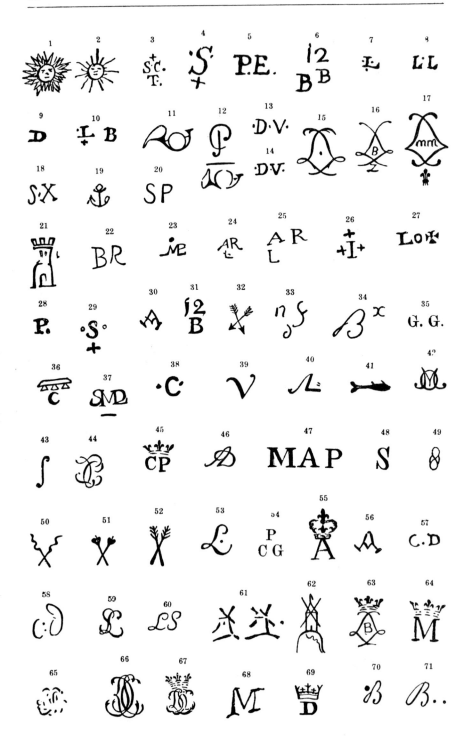

EARLY FRENCH PORCELAIN MARKS

1-6. Marks resembling works of St. Cloud.

7-10. Marks resembling LILLE.

11-12. CHANTILLY.

13-14. MENNECY-VILLEROY in gold, later this was impressed.

15-17. VINCENNES (early Sevres).

18-20. SCEAUX.

21. LA TOUR D'AIGUES.

22. BOURG LA REINE. Established 1773.

23-25. ARRAS.

26-35. Attributed to ST. CLOUD.

36. ORLEANS.

37-43. FONTAINEBLEAU.

44-52. PARIS. Jacob Pettit was among the most famous Paris factories.

53-56. PARIS. Established 1790. Made hard-paste, made a large variety of beautiful wares.

59-60. LA SIENIE. Established 1774.

61-69. CLIGNANCOURT.

70-71. BOISSETTE, Established 1777.

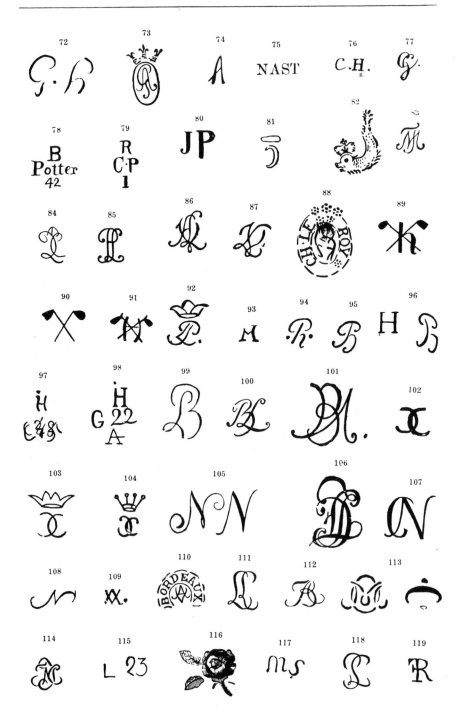

EARLY FRENCH PORCELAIN MARKS

72-81. PARIS.

82. LILLE.

83-85. PARIS.

86-87. VALENCIENNES.

88. CHOISY-le-ROI. Established 1786.

89-92. VINCENNES. Established by Pierre Antoine Hannong, 1786.

93-98. STRASSBOURG. Paul Hannong had a factory here about 1750, later learned the secret of hard-paste porcelain, but before he could make the wares, was forced to suspend his works, and later went to Frankenthal.

99. BRANCAS LAURAGAIS.

100. ORLEANS.

101-108. NIDERVILLER. These marks are often confused with marks of Ludwigsburg. The name NIDERVILLER is often impressed on Bisque figures. These are especially on pieces related to historical American figures such as Franklin, Washington, etc.

109-110. BORDEAUX. Marks of Verneulle.

111. Unknown. Resembles mark used by Limbach (Germany).

112-118. Unidentified French porcelain marks.

119. MARSEILLES.
This was at a period when both soft and hard-paste porcelain ware were first used all over Europe. Many factories were opened by royalty as a sort of hobby, and of course closed very soon; others remained, and copied each other's marks and designs. It is very hard to sometimes distinguish many of them for this reason.

1 Matthias Rosa im. Anspach

2 B.B.

3 BK / C

4 B P

5 BP B·P ·BP

6 ‡

7 M

8 A / F

9 H

10 göggingen HS

11 S.

12 G

13 jZ

14 ⊛

15 ⚓

16 G:Koxdenbusch.

17 GK:.

18 A

19 NB. / K:·   NB / F   NB:· / 4.

20 Stebner 1775 d.13 8bris

21 S

22 WE / u &

23 F. 20 / 7   E   68.P.F.   Hm

24 D. 11 / 4 -10   E

25 A / P / MR

26 B / S

27 DP / 53X

28 F.B.C.F. 1779

29 GHEDT W:I:M JT30

30 JE JA

31 H / G

32 :HS:

33 JKR N

34 HN XX   HN XX

35 J

36 R / N

37 oTF

38 F. Pahl. .Nō.:1796.:

39 PH

40 N Pössimoer Anno 1725

41 R / M / 67

42 R·M / E

43 S.

44 JKB B

45 VH / 3

46 W

47 Y

1. ANSPACH. Signature of artist, ware resembling Rouen.

2-6. BAIREUTH. Began to make pottery here during the 16th century.

7-9. FRANKENTHAL. Marks used by Paul Hannong and son, on their pottery.

10. GOGGINGEN. 1750, a potter began making pottery here. His initial, H.R., is the only sign of his name.

11. HARBURG. Johann Schaper, during 1620 to 1670, famous for his exquisite painting on glass, his pottery mugs were also painted with the most painstaking details.

12-14. HÖCHST, first made pottery 1720, by Geltz. Its porcelain products soon became famous, and overshadowed the pottery.

15. POPPELSDORF.

16-20. NUREMBERG.

21. SCHREITZHEIM. Generations of fine pottery was made by the family "Wintergurst," from 1620, to the present time. Of course porcelain is now made.

22-24. STRALSUND, 1738.

25-47. Marks of unknown German Origin.

1-8. MEISSEN, also known as DRESDEN. This is the first marks on Böttcher's "red ware," as his first pieces are commonly known. This was very early in the 18th century. This was a chocolate like color, well made and decorated with Chinese designs in gold and silver colorings. It is of interest to note that the very first marks of Böttcher were copies of Chinese.

9-11. BÖTTCHER, had now stumbled on the discovery of true porcelain making, and used the initials of Augustus Rex, elector of Saxony, under whose patronage he worked. Böttcher led a very fast life, as we would call it today, he was continually drunk, fond of night life, and a continuous drinker. However he combined this with being a hard worker, for he did indeed discover hard porcelain, and then soon died.

12-13. First marks on articles offered for sale at the Leipzig Fair. 1717-20.

14-15. KING'S PERIOD.

16. CROSS SWORD, with star, Prof. Marcolini period.

17-18. Early mark of MEISSENER PORZELLAN MANUFACTUR.

19. First form of cross swords 1719.

20. Mark of 1720.

21. Dresden mark during "Bruhl's period" 1750.

22. Cross sword used about 1850.

23. Used 1860.

24. Mark used on pieces made specially for Countess Cosel.

25-33. Early marks used on Dresden 1718-1740.

34-38. Marks of various workers of the Höchst factories. These factories were later destroyed by the French in 1794, and then discontinued. Later Mr. Dahl got control of the moulds and continued to operate for a while. Mr. Melchior was the best workman employed at the early Höchst works, and his work for quality and modelling has never been equalled even in modern times.

39-40. FÜRSTENBERG. Established in 1750, by ex-workmen of the Höchst works.

41. HESSE CASSEL.

42. HESSE DARMSTADT.

43-44. FULDA. Established 1763, produced fine vases, figures, and service. Well decorated, good specimens are rare, and highly prized.

45-47. GOTHA. Founded 1780, by Rothenburg.

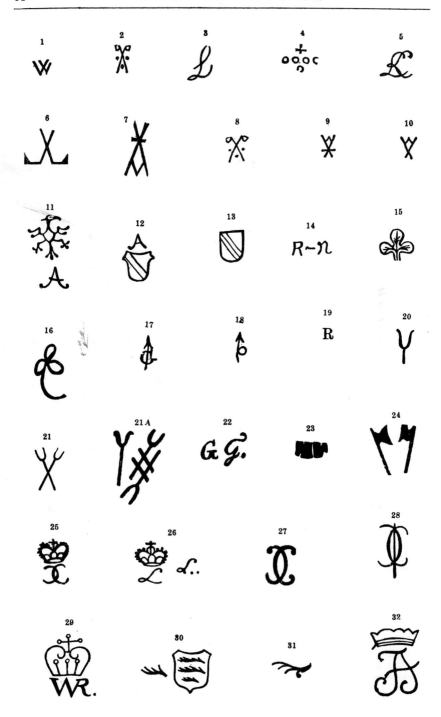

1. WALLENDORF. Established by Macheleidt, under the patronage of the Prince of Schwarzburg, 1762. In 1770 the factory passed into the hands of G. Greiner.

2. ARNSTADT. F. G. Feigel, a decorator established in 1770.

3-6. LIMBACH. Established by Macheleidt, 1761, also passed into the hands of G. Greiner.

7-13. ANSPACH. Since 1806, this town in Bavaria is the seat of the hard paste porcelain industry; some very fine art objects are made here.

14. RAUENSTEIN. Established 1760, its products resemble those of the Wallendorf factory, as they were the same owners.

15-18. GROSBREITENBACH. These marks are also of the same owners as the Wallendorf factory, works are similar.

19-21a. RUDOLSTADT. Same owners as the Wallendorf factory, established about the same time.

22. GERA. Also various other forms of "G," established 1780, first copied Chinese and then other German wares.

23-24. BADEN-BADEN. Mark usually printed or impressed, established 1753 by the widow Sperl.

25-31. LUDWIGSBURG. Ringler established a factory here in 1758, this is one of the foremost factories in Germany today, only second to that at Dresden, and Berlin, and is certainly not second to any factory with regards to its products.

32. HILDESCHEIM. Letter "A" alone also used.

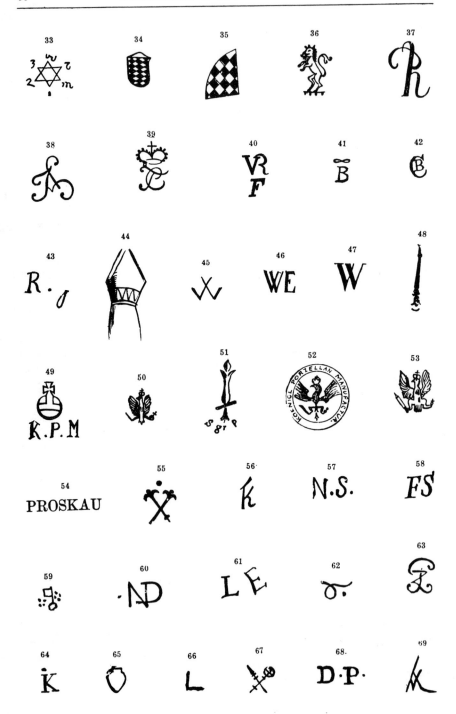

33-35. NYMPHENBERG. These marks were often impressed without color, and are difficult to recognize, founded in 1747, Mr. Ringler became head man in 1756. Undecorated pieces were often sold to other factories for decorations. So these pieces often have 2 marks of 2 distinctive factories on them.

36-41. FRANKENTHAL. Founded by Paul Hannong, who formerly had a factory in France, in 1754, this firm made wares of the highest merit until 1800. In 1761 the factory became under the patronage of Elector Carl Theodore. Its wares are of unsurpassed merit, its figures and decorations second to none. The works were sold in 1800 to private hands and was moved to Greinstadt.

42. BAIREUTH. 19th century.

43. REGENSBURG. Founded 1760 by the same owners as of the Wallendorf.

44. WURTZBURG.

45-50. ROYAL BERLIN. Established 1751, by Wm. Wegeley, the mark "W" are on early specimens. In 1761 the factory was purchased by Gottskowski, and greatly improved its products. After the occupation of Dresden by Frederick the Great, he removed the Meissen factory, lock, stock, and barrel to Berlin, that is raw material, moulds, and workmen, and of course their wares increased in beauty until they were the best in Germany. This factory has achieved the greatest advance of ceramic art on the continent. A decree issued by Frederick forbade any Jew in his kingdom to marry, unless he purchased a said amount of porcelain from his factory. This of course was done to encourage the sale of its output.

51-52. ROYAL BERLIN. This is a special mark for soft paste, No. 52, a late mark.

53. CHARLOTTENBERG. Founded 1760, by Pressel, and continued until absorbed by the Royal Berlin works.

55-57. UNKNOWN GERMAN PORCELAIN MARKS.

58-69. UNKNOWN GERMAN PORCELAIN MARKS.

1-2. NORDDEUTCHE STEINGUTTFABRIK. Established 1870.

3-5. Unknown German marks.

6. ANNABURG. Established 1874.

7. ARNOLDI. Established by C. & F. Arnoldi about 1808.

8. BAENSCH. At Lettin, established 1858.

9. MADGEBURG-NUESTADT. Established 1865 by Adolf Bauer.

10. Unknown.

11-12. BENEDIKT BROS. Established 1884.

13. BERTRAM BERHARD LUFTELBURG.

14. Unknown.

15. BORDOLLO BROS. GRUNSTADT.

16. Unknown.

17. BUCKAUER PORZ. Established 1833.

18-20. Unknown.

21. DAEHMEL. Established 1854.

22-24. Unknown.

25. EISENBERGER.

26. Unknown.

27-29. PIRKENHAMMER. No. 29, latest mark.

30. FRANKE A. Near Dresden, established 1840.

31. TILLOWITZ.

32-43. MISCELLANEOUS MARKS ON GERMAN PORCELAIN.

1

2   Schwaz

3

4

5

6   JACOBI ADLER + Cᵒ   NEULEININGEN

7   Rheinsberg

8

9

10

11

12   Miskolez

13   M K

14   CHINA   K P M

15   Royal   1755   Bonn

16   FRANZ ANT. MEHLEM   BONN a/RHEIN

17   R H

18   GERMANY   RW   RUDOLSTADT

19   CROWN   RW   RUDOLSTADT

20

21   SAXE

22   H P & Cie   Kolmar

23   K&G   PRAG

24   THEODOR PAETSCH   FRANKFURT A/M

25

26   G

27

28   P L

29   VICTORIA   KARLSBAD   AUSTRIA

1. HUBBE BROS. Established 1875.
2. HUSSL J. Established 1801, specialized in Oriental style wares.
3. C. M. HUTSCHENDREUTHER. Established 1814, made blanks for decorators, with blue Vienna mark under glaze.
4-5. Unknown.
6. JACOBI ADLER & CO. Established 1874. Grundtadt.
7. G. JACKSON. Rheinsburg. Established 1815.
8-9. Unknown.
10. Marseille Armand. Established 1865.
11. KONIGLICH BAYERISCHE PORZ. Manufactured set 1757, near Munich.
12. MAX KOOS. Miskolez. Established 1882.
13. R. KRAUSE. Established 1882.
14. C. KRISTER. Imitated Royal Berlin wares.
15-16. ROYAL BONN. Made many vases, service and other ornaments similar to pieces made by the Doulton and Worcester works. Its wares are often sold as English.
17. German mark used on vases, figures and ornaments sold as English.
18-19. L. STRAUSS & SONS. New York importing house established a factory in Germany, which became one of the largest in the world; service, statues bisque, ornaments and other porcelain wares were produced in huge quantities. These pieces were never too fine, and were made chiefly for middle class trade. The designs and motifs were usually copies of better known makers. Some of the vases and figures made here have received recognition due to their high quality floral work, and finely executed bisque statues.
20-28. Miscellaneous late Austrian and German marks.
29. LAZARUS ROSENFELD. Of New York, established a factory at Carlsbad.

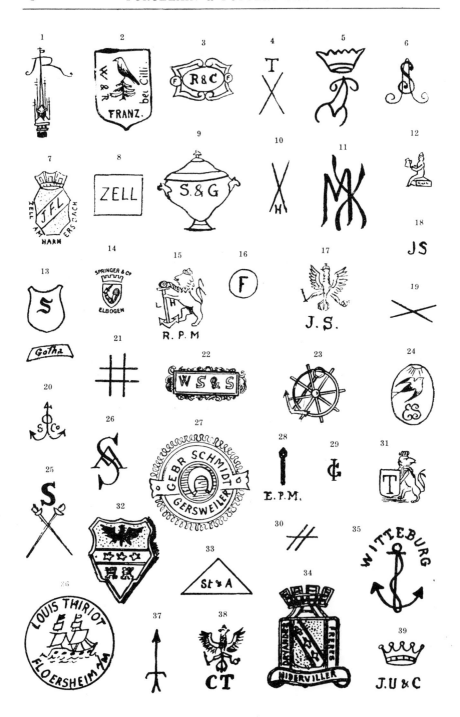

1. PEPOVECKI S. Established 1835, at Znaim. Specialized in majolica type wares.

2. REISSBERGER & CO. Established 1882.

3. RISSLER & CO. Freiburg, established 1847.

4. CARL THIEME. Potschappel.

5. Copy on imitation of Capo-di-Monte, made by Carl Thieme.

6. A. SALTZER. Eisenbach, established 1858.

7-8. CARL SCHAAF. Established 1807.

9. SCHEMLZER & GERICKE. Established 1865.

10. ALBERT SCHMIDT. Established 1863.

11. SCHMIDT GEBRUDER. Established 1847.

12. H. SCHMIDT. Established 1842.

13. GOTHA. Established by Rothenber, 1767.

14. SPRINGER & CO. Elbogen, established 1815, possessed one of the largest kilns in the world. One of the world's largest independent firms.

15-31. Marks of small independent porcelain works in Germany.

32. J. VON SCHWARZ. Majolica wares.

33. STEINER & ADLER. Established 1889.

34. STEINGUTFABRIK NEIDERWELLER. Established 1750.

35. WITTEBURG.

36. LOUIS THIRIOT. Florscheim, small but important factory.

37-39. Small independent German manufacturers.

1-7. UTZCHNEIDER & CO. Sarreguemines. Established 1770, also operate a factory at Degoin, France. Make a large variety of service and porcelain objects.

9-11. Unknown German porcelain marks.

12. LUDWIG WESSELL. Ornamental vases.

13. GILHEMSBURGER STEINGUTTFABRIK. Established 1835.

14. WITTENBERGER. Established 1884.

15. TEPLITZ. Established by Ernest Wahleiss. Specialized in figures, vases, and ornamental objects.

16-17. Unknown.

18. ZSOLNAY, at Funfkirchen. Established 1885, unusually highly glazed and enamelled wares, soft paste wares. Their works are usually highly perforated, and highly enamelled in many colors which are brilliant. These pieces are in strong demand at present.

19-22. Royal Vienna. Claude Innocent du Pasquier went to Dresden, and bribed some ex-workmen of the Meissen plant to leave, and then established the works in Vienna under the patronage of the royal ruling house of Austria. As the workmen were poorly paid, they did not communicate the secret to Pasquier, and the products were poor, and the factory closed. However, Pasquier experimented and soon he discovered the secret of the manufacture of porcelain. The articles produced are among the finest in the world. Expert chemists were employed to obtain the most brilliant colors. The gilding on these pieces have world renown. The painting of Watteau, Boucher, and Angelica Kauffman, have been expertly produced on vases, plates and plaques of "Royal Vienna." However, due to the financial loss under which this factory operated the works were abandoned in 1864. "Royal Vienna" is among the most counterfeited marks, for during the past 25 years more so-called "Royal Vienna" marked pieces were sold than during the entire existence of the "Royal Vienna" factory before they suspended operations.

23-25. SCHLAKENWALD.

26-31. HEREND. Sometimes impressed or painted. Sometimes M.F., which stands for Moritz Fischer, are of different size. This factory produced much ware, copying wares of France, England, and Germany, and even Chinese products. So good was the copying that it has been very difficult to determine. One such copy found its way into South Kensington Museum, as a Chinese product.

32-33. ALTEN ROTHAU.

34. PRAGUE.

1-10. Villeroy & Boch. Marks used before 1800.

11-13. Used after 1800 to 1832.

14-35. Used on wares made by Villeroy & Boch, and known as METTLACH.

36. Used on wares made especially for Hamburger & Co.

37-38. BAWO & DOTTER. Fischern.

39. C. L. DWENGER.

40-41. PORZELLAN FABRIK KLOESTERLE. Output controlled by Bawo & Dotter.

42-44. Wares made especially for AHRENFELDT & SON, of New York. These products were made at various Austrian factories.

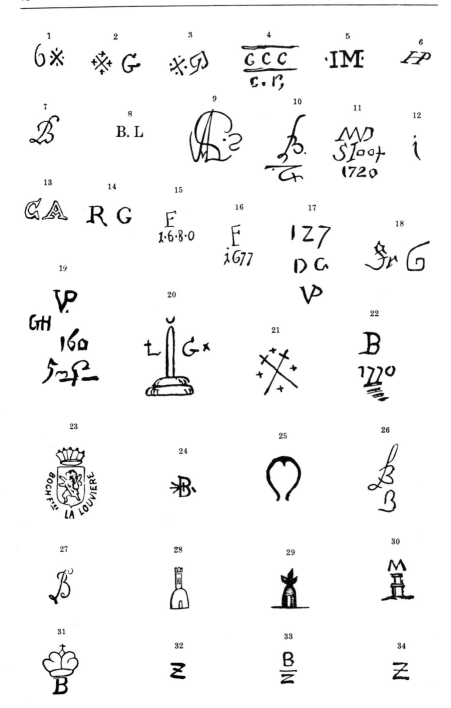

1-3. TOURNAY. Attributed to Peternyck.

4. TERVUEREN.

5. MALINES.

6. HENRI PULINX (BRUGES).

7. LUXEMBOURG BOCH BROS. Prior to French Revolution.

8. Same but impressed.

9-10. LUXEMBOURG.

11-19. Unknown marks attributed to French potters.

20. LIEGE. Established 1752, works continued for 15 years, and then closed. Their works were principally copies of other factories.

21-22. TOURNAY. Established early 18th century. Later many Englishmen were employed here to decorate. Made wares similar to Sevres.

23-24. BOCH BROS.

25. BRUGES.

26-27. LUXEMBOURG.

28-30. TOURNAY.

31. BRUSSELS.

32-34. ZURICH.

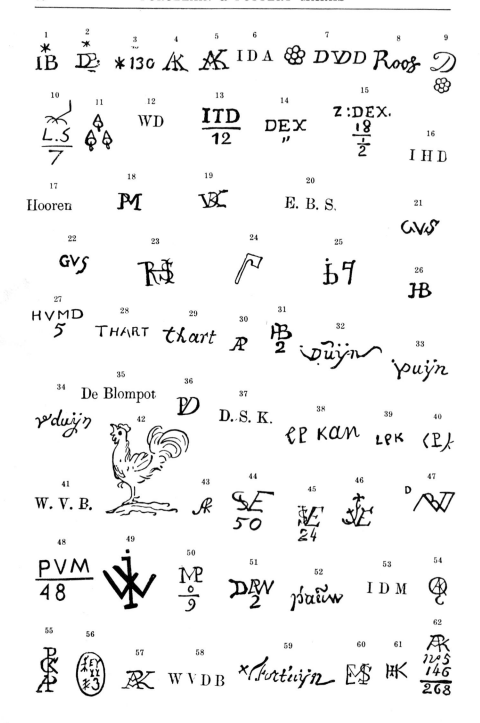

1-5. DE WITTE STER (The White Star). A. Kielle.

6. IN DER VERGULDE BOOR (The Gilded Boat). Johannes de Appel.

7-9. DE ROOS (The Rose). Dirk Van Der Does.

10. DE KLAAUW (The Claw). Lambertus Sanderus.

11-12. DE DRIE KLOKKEN (The Three Bells). W. Van der Does.

13-16. DE GRIEKSE (The Greek). J. T. Dextra, later J. H. Adriaensz.

17. DE DRIE PORCELEYNE ASTONNEN (The Three Porcelain Barrels). Hendrik Van Hoorn.

18-19. DE ROMEYN (The Roman). Petrus Van Marum.

20. T'JOGNUE MORIAANS HOFFT (The Young Moor's Head).

21-23. IN TOUDE MORIAANS HOFFT (The Old Moor's Head).

24-25. DE PORCELEIN BYL (The Porcelain Hatcher). Justus Brouwer.

26-27. DE DRIE PORELEYNE FLESCHJES (The Three Porcelain Bottles).

28-30. T'HART (The Stag). Hendrik Van Middeldyk.

31. DE TWEE SCHEEPJES (The Two Ships). Anth. Pennis.

32-34. DE PORCELEYNE SCHOOTEL (The Porcelain Dish). Johannes Van Duyn.

35. DE VERGULDE BLOMPOT (The Gilded Flowerpot).

36. DE PORELEYNE FLES (The Porcelain Bottle). Peter van Doorne.

37. DE DUBBELDE SCHENKAN (The Double Pitcher). Thomas Spaandonek.

38-40. DE LAMPETKAN (The Ewer).

41. DE TWE WILDEMANS (The Two Savages). Widow of Willem van Beek.

42. AMSTERDAM. 1780.

43-62. MAKERS OF DELFT POTTERY.

$\cancel{B}$ $\dfrac{A}{D}{12}$ $\mathcal{K}$ AK $\dot{A}\dot{K}$ AP $\dfrac{AV}{27\frac{1}{2}}{0}$ $A\mathcal{V}\,3{-}2\,\Upsilon$

$\cdot\dot{B}\cdot$ $\underline{B}$ BVD $\underset{0}{\overset{15}{C}}$ $\mathcal{C}\,|\,\overset{a}{\mathcal{C}}$ $\underset{N\Lambda.}{\mathcal{E}}$

F^{DH} $\mathfrak{fi}$ $\dfrac{GB}{+}{X}$ $\overline{\mathcal{FK}}$ $\mathcal{GB}$ $\dfrac{HDK}{3}$ H:G EG 1732

$\underset{NVG.}{\mathcal{h.}}$ H PI $\overset{*}{iB}$ $\overset{*}{JB}$ $\underset{2G}{iG}$ ID W

$\dot{k}\,\overset{*}{K}$ $\dot{P}$ $\overset{V\!B}{VE\mathcal{I}}$ J_{VOH} $\{VH$ $\dfrac{JG}{22\frac{1}{2}}$

$\underline{J\mathcal{E}}$ $\dfrac{V}{2}{4}$ $\dot{V}$ MVB 1757   KF   VA

K:D: GK   .MK.   P.

                  $\underline{PVB}$

$\mathcal{P\cdot V\cdot D\cdot S}$ $\dfrac{P}{if}$ R $\dfrac{9}{18}$ $\underset{N:380}{V}$
$A^\circ\mathcal{J}1754.$

            $\mathcal{R}$ P VS WVS 1717

$\overset{VA}{F_1}$ $\overset{V}{2}E_2$ $\underset{DS}{V\frac{1}{2}E}$ VVK   WK

Unknown marks on Dutch pottery.

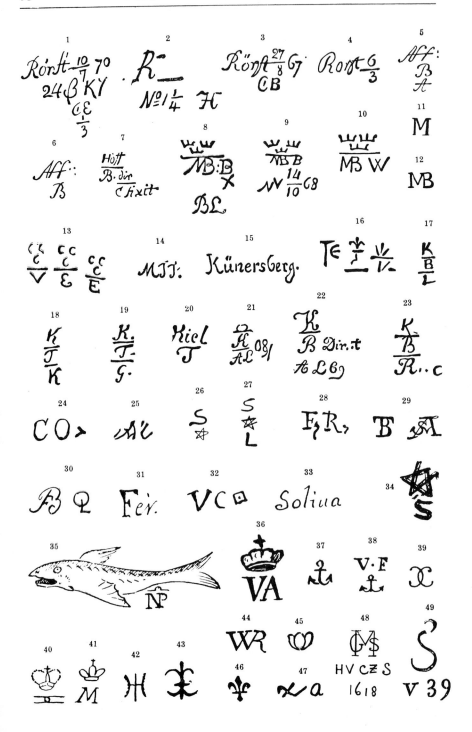

1-6. Early marks of RORSTRAND. Established 1727.

7. Unknown Swedish mark.

8-13. MARIEBERG. Early marks, probably about 1758. The factory was established 1750, by Queen Louisa Ulrika, whose brother was Frederick the Great of Prussia.

Good quality pottery and porcelain was made here, and the factory continued to operate under the direction of Dr. Ehrenreich, and was closed in 1780.

14. SWEDISH MARK.

15-16. KUNERSBERG.

17-23. KIEL

24-25. ALCORA (Spain).

26-27. SEVILLE.

28-29. PORTUGUESE MARKS.

30-33. ALCORA, Spain. Founded 1727, by a Spanish nobleman who employed French workmen. Articles made here resembled French products. Plaques of religious nature were also made.

34-35. SEVILLE.

36. VISTA ALLEGRE (Portugal). Established 1790.

37-43. BUEN RETIRO, Madrid. This was the foremost of the Spanish porcelain factories. These were owned by the state, employees were pledged to secrecy, and the public were not permitted to see or visit this factory. Workmen of the Capo-di-Monte factory were employed here, and the works closely resembled these wares. The factory, however, was destroyed during the Spanish Peninsular War of 1812. Marks also resembled the Capo-di-Monte.

44-49. Unknown marks, now believed German.

1-2. COPENHAGEN. Early mark. This factory, like many others of this period was founded by the King of Denmark, 1772, who employed ex-workmen of the Dresden works. Naturally the first pieces made were articles similar to the Dresden factories. Later, however, this factory made works all of its own character, chiefly modeling figures of animals and birds, in natural color, and extraordinarily fine. Fine statuary and groups were also made, together with service. Everyone should be familiar with the Copenhagen style animals and figures, and need no further description of them here.

3. Later mark.

4. B. & G. Impressed or printed, this is a factory organized recently at Copenhagen, which also makes a similar type ware, which, however, is not as fine as the Royal Copenhagen.

5. ROYAL ST. PETERSBURGH. Organized about 1741, with French workmen.

6-7. Time of Empress Catherine, 1762.

8. Mark of Paul, 1798.

9. Alexander, 1801.

10. Nicholas, 1825.

11-12. Alexander 2nd, 1855.

13. System of dots arranged so that each year after 1871 a dot appears. One dot for 1871, two dots for 1872, and etc.

14-15. THE BROTHERS KORNILOFF. St. Petersburg.

16-19. GARDNER. Moscow.

20. BARANOWKA. Poland.

21-24. MOSCOW.

25-26. KIEV.

27. CHMELOFF. Poland.

28. KORZEC. Poland.

1-31. BOW CHINA WORKS. Established 1740, most of the Bow marks are doubtful, but are generally accepted. The Bow factory was purchased by Mr. Duesbury in 1775, who transferred the moulds and formulas to the Derby works.

32-46. CHELSEA. Established 1745, the anchor is considered the true Chelsea mark; it is either embossed or painted. During this early period many factories copied each other's marks, so that it is most difficult to tell true Chelsea. For the past 100 years many of the English and especially German factories have copied the anchor symbol, so that it makes this symbol very common. Many figures and vases and other ornaments appear to have this mark, but it seldom is true Chelsea. The chief reason for this is that this factory also was sold to Mr. Duesbury, who continued for a short while, and then closed it, after bringing the moulds and workmen to his plant at Derby in 1784.

47-48. CAUGHLEY (later known as COALPORT). These first marks, such as the crescent, was also used by the Worcester works, the mark of "C" and "S," later adopted. This firm was founded in 1750.

49-61. Later marks of Caughley.

62-64. Mark of COALPORT. This firm is well known for their jewel like type of porcelain, its works are indeed beautiful and have great artistic merit, and greatly sought after.

ALPHABETICAL LIST OF NAMES AND INITIALS FOUND ON ENGLISH WARES.

Adams (William)—Tunstall, Staffordshire; 18th century.

Adams, J.—Tunstall, Staffordshire; 18th century.

Aynsley, J.—Lane End, Staffordshire; 18th century.

Bailey and Batkin—La End, Staffordshire; 19th century.

Birch—Staffordshire; 18th century.

Booth, Enoch—Tunstall; 18th century.

Bolt and Co.—Staffordshire.

Bournes Potteries — Belper and Denby, Derbyshire; 18th and 19th centuries.

Brameld—Rockingham; 19th century.

Bridgwood and Son—Staffordshire; 19th century.

Bulkeley and Bent—Staffordshire; 18th century.

C. and G. (Copeland and Garret)—Stoke-upon-Trent; 19th century.

C. G. (Charles Green) — Leeds, Yorkshire; 18th century.

C. and H. (Cookson and Harding)—Staffordshire; 18th century.

Cadogan — Rockingham, Yorkshire; 18th and 19th centuries.

Chaffers, Richard—Liverpool; 18th century.

Child—Tunstall, Staffordshire; 18th century.

Clews—Cobridge, Staffordshire; 18th century.

Close and Co.—Hanley, Staffordshire; 18th century.

Copeland—Stoke-upon-Trent, Staffordshire; 19th century.

Copeland, late Spode — Stoke-upon-Trent, Staffordshire; 19th century.

Crystal ware—Staffordshire; 18th century.

D. D. and Co. (David Dunderdale and Co.)—Castleford, Yorkshire; 18th and 19th centuries.

Dawson—Sunderland; 19th century.

Dillwyn and Co.—Swansea; 19th century.

Dixon, Austin, and Co. — Sunderland; 19th century.

Don Pottery — Doncaster, Yorkshire; 18th and 19th centuries.

1-2. Early mark, generally attributed to Derby. This firm was founded in 1751, by Wm. Duesbury. The work did not become famous until after the purchasing of the Chelsea factory. Mr. Duesbury died, 1788, and his son succeeded him, having as a partner Mr. Michael Kean, who managed the works after the death of young Duesbury. In 1815 these were sold to Robert Bloor, who managed to hold the works until his death, 1849, and then passed to new owner again, after several more owners they passed to the hands of Mr. Hancock in 1866.

3-4. First period about 1768.

5-48. Other Derby marks until 1898.

49. Special Derby mark on pieces made for the Persian Ambassador.

50. Mark used on plate of same.

51. Mark used in 1842, on imitations of Sevres.

52-65. Mark used by various artists employed by the Derby works. Most famous is that of Mr. Cocker, 60-64. No. 65 is another mark used on copies of Sevres.

ALPHABETICAL LIST OF NAMES AND INITIALS FOUND ON ENGLISH WARES.

Doulton—Lambeth; 18th and 19th centuries.

Dudson—Staffordshire; 18th century.

Dwight, J.—Fulham; 17th and 18th centuries.

Eastwood—Staffordshire; 18th century.

Elers—Staffordshire; 17th and 18th centuries.

F. G.—Uncertain.

Fell—Newcastle-upon-Tyne · 18th and 19th centuries.

Fell and Co.—Newcastle-upon-Tyne; 19th century.

Freeling and Co.—Staffordshire.

Fulham Pottery—Fulham; 19th century.

Gordon, R. G.—Staffordshire; 18th century.

G. (Green)—Leeds, Yorkshire; 18th century.

Ḡ. and crown—Leeds, Yorkshire; 18th century.

Green, Don Pottery — Doncaster, Staffordshire; 18th century.

Green, Stephen—Lambeth; 18th and 19th centuries.

Gunther and Co., S. B. B.—Staffordshire? (Probably not potters.)

H. and S.—Uncertain—Staffordshire?

Hackwood—Shelton, Staffordshire; 18th century.

Hackwood and Co.—Shelton, Staffordshire; 19th century.

Harding—Staffordshire; 18th century.

Harley, T.—Lane End, Staffordshire; 18th century.

Harrison, G.—Staffordshire; 18th century.

Hartley, Greens, and Co.—Leeds, Yorkshire; 18th century.

Heath—Staffordshire; 18th century.

Herculaneum—Liverpool; 18th and 19th centuries.

Hollins, S.—Shelton, Staffordshire; 18th century.

Hollins, T. and J.—Shelton, Staffordshire; 18th century.

I. E. B.—Uncertain.

J. Y. (J. Yates)—Staffordshire; 18th century.

Jobson—Staffordshire; 18th century.

Keeling, J.—Hanley, Staffordshire; 18th century.

Lakin—Staffordshire; 18th century.

Lakin and Poole—Staffordshire; 18th century.

Leeds Pottery—Leeds, Yorkshire; 18th century.

Lockett, J.—Lane End, Staffordshire; 18th century.

Lowesby—Leicestershire; 19th century.

M., and a number (Thomas Miles)—Staffordshire; 18th and 19th centuries.

M. N. (Mayer and Newbold)—Staffordshire; 18th century.

Marshall and Co.—Staffordshire; 18th century.

Mason, M.—Lane Delph, Staffordshire; 18th and 19th centuries.

Mason's patent Iron-stone China — Lane Delph, Staffordshire: 18th and 19th centuries.

1-8. DAVENPORT. Established at Longport, 1794, and was famous for the fine service produced here. In 1872 the firm ceased to exist.

9-10. J. EDWARDS. Fenton.

11. D. CHAPMAN. Longton fine Chinawares.

12. R. CHAFFERS. Liverpool, 18th century potter.

13-14. Wm. Adderly & Co. Longton. Established 1870.

15. GEORGE ASHWORTH & BROS. Hanley.

16. J. & G. ALCOCK. Cobridge. Much of these wares were sold to America.

17. HENRY ALCOCK & CO. Cobridge.

18-19. BELLEEK. Established 1863, by McBirney & Armstrong, this was the first firm to make a very fine eggshell-like porcelain with a high iridescent lustre, many American firms imitated these wares.

20-22. BELLEVUE POTTERY. Hull. Established 1802 by Job Ridgway.

23. ISAAC BAGULEY. A decorator formerly employed by the Derby Works, and later with the Rockingham works, commenced to operate successfully in 1842. He used the Rockingham seal, and sometimes signed his name over the Rockingham seal.

24-26. S. BARKER & SONS. Also known as the Don Pottery at Swinton, a fine line of decorated and perforated wares were made of soft paste porcelain. DON POTTERY is sometimes impressed. This firm established in early part of the 19th century.

27-28. E. J. D. BODLEY. Hanley. Chinawares.

29. E. F. BODLEY & CO. Burslem.

30-33. T. & R. BOOTE. Burslem. Established late 18th century.

34-42. BRAMELS & CO. Known as the Rockingham works, this firm was founded late 18th century, and closed 1842. They made articles of great artistic beauty and merit, but did not operate financially well. The name MORTLOCK, and CADOGANS ROCKINGHAM, and MORTLOCK'S CADOGAN, are sometimes impressed in their china. During Jefferson's administration a service for the White House was made here.

ALPHABETICAL LIST OF NAMES AND INITIALS FOUND ON ENGLISH WARES.

Mason's Cambrian Argil—Lane Delph, Staffordshire; 18th and 19th centuries.

Mayer, E., Hanley—Staffordshire; 18th century.

Mayer, Joseph, and Co.— Hanley, Staffordshire; 18th century.

Meigh—Hanley, Staffordshire; 18th and 19th centuries

Meigh, J., and Sons—Hanley, Staffordshire; 18th and 19th centuries.

Miles—Hanley, Staffordshire; 18th century.

Milson—Bristol; 19th century.

Minton—Stoke-upon-Trent, Staffordshire; 18th and 19th centuries.

1-3. SAMPSON BRIDGWOOD & SON. Longton.

4. JAMES BEECH. Tunstall.

5. BATES, ELLIOTT & CO. Established 1790.

6-22. BRISTOL. One of the first English porcelain factories, originally made pottery and then porcelain. This firm was established 1703, and after 100 years ceased to exist. Like many firms of this time they copied each other's wares and marks, so that the marks of Dresden and Bristol are very similar.

23-24. Marks of decorators employed at the Bristol works.

25. J. & G. ALCOCK. Cobridge. Established 1843.

26-30. COBRIDGE WORKS. This factory founded by Stevenson & Dale, 1780, and after several other partners the factory closed in 1836. The factory reopened and after several other owners W. Brownfield & Son became sole owner. After several years this factory became known as BROWNFIELD GUILD POTTERIES.

31-32. Marks of the Brownfield group.

33-34. E. BOURNE. Burslem.

35-36. BOOTHS. Tunstall.

37. BROWN WESTHEAD, MOORE & CO. Stoke on Trent. This firm makes the well known Cauldon china, and is one of the foremost English companies today. Started by Job Ridgway, 1794, and continued to operate by sons of Ridgway until 1860, when Mr. Brown-Westhead became owner with Mr. Moore as his partner. Everything in the line of fine china and porcelain is made here.

38-39. Early marks on Historical American Plates.

40-41. Later marks.

42-44. Marks to 1898.

ALPHABETICAL LIST OF NAMES AND INITIALS FOUND ON ENGLISH WARES.

Minton and Boyle—Stoke-upon-Trent, Staffordshire; 18th and 19th centuries.

Mist, London—Staffordshire; 18th century.

Moore and Co.—Southwick; 18th and 19th centuries.

Mortlock Cadogan—Rockingham, Yorkshire; 19th century.

Moseley—Staffordshire; 18th century.

Myat, T.—Lane Delph, Staffordshire; 18th century.

Neale, J. Hanley—Hanley, Staffordshire; 18th century.

Neale and Co.—Hanley, Staffordshire; 18th century.

Neale and Wilson—Hanley, Staffordshire; 18th century.

Neeld—Staffordshire; 18th century.

Nell—Staffordshire; 18th century.

Newcastle—Newcastle; 18th and 19th centuries.

Opaque Porcelain—Swansea; 19th century.

P. (Pennington)—Liverpool; 18th century.

Palmer, Hanley—Hanley, Staffordshire; 18th century.

Palmer and Neale—Hanley, Staffordshire; 18th century.

Palmer and Voyez—Hanley, Staffordshire; 18th century.

Pearl-ware—Lane End (Messrs. Cheatham and Wooley), Staffordshire; 18th century.

1-6. W. COCKWORTHY. Plymouth. Known as PLYMOUTH WARE. Mr. Cockworthy was a chemist, who was the first Englishman to make true porcelain, 1760, and had much litigation regarding the patent. He sold his factory and came to America.

7-37. W. T. COPELAND & SONS. Also known as SPODE. The firm was founded in 1770, by J. Spode, and later Mr. Copeland became partner. The firm became very successful, and is still among the foremost English companies.

38-43. COLEBROOK-DALE. First three are older marks, later three are marks after 1851.

44. SHELTON. Also known as "NEW HALL."

45-49. PINXTON.

ALPHABETICAL LIST OF NAMES AND INITIALS FOUND ON ENGLISH WARES.

Phillips, E.—Longport, Staffordshire; 18th century.

Plant, B.—Lane End, Staffordshire; 18th century.

Poole, R.—Staffordshire; 18th century.

Pratt, F. and R. and Co.—Fenton, Staffordshire; 19th century.

Richus and Toft—Staffordshire; 19th century.

Ridgway—Shelton, Staffordshire; 18th and 19th centuries.

Ridgway and Sons—Shelton, Staffordshire; 18th and 19th centuries.

Riley's Semi-china—Staffordshire; 19th century.

Rockingham—Yorkshire; 18th and 19th centuries.

Rogers—Staffordshire; 18th century.

S. (Salopian)—Caughley, Shropshire; 18th and 19th centuries.

S. and B.—Sibury and Bridgwood, Staffordshire; 19th century.

S. and Co. (J. Shore and Co.)—Isleworth; 19th century.

Sadler—Liverpool; 18th century.

Sadler and Green—Liverpool; 18th century.

Salopian—Caughley, Shropshire; 18th and 19th centuries.

Salt—Staffordshire; 18th century.

Sans, William—Staffordshire; 17th century.

Scott—Sunderland; 18th and 19th centuries.

Sewell—Sunderland; 18th and 19th centuries.

Sewell and Donkin—Sunderland; 18th and 19th centuries.

Sewells and Co.—Sunderland; 18th and 19th centuries.

Sharpe—Swadlincote, Burton-on-Trent; 19th century.

Shorthose—Staffordshire; 18th and 19th centuries.

Shorthose and Co.—Staffordshire; 18th and 19th centuries.

Shorthose and Heath—Staffordshire; 18th and 19th centuries.

Sneyd, T.—Hanley, Staffordshire; 19th century.

Snitzer—Lambeth; 18th century.

Spode—Stoke-upon-Trent, Staffordshire; 18th and 19th centuries.

Spode, Felspar porcelain—Stoke-upon-Trent, Staffordshire; 18th and 19th centuries.

Spode, Son, and Copeland—Stoke-upon-Trent, Staffordshire; 18th and 19th centuries.

Steel—Burslem, Staffordshire; 18th century.

Stephenson, A.—Staffordshire; 18th century.

Swansea—18th and 19th centuries.

Swansea, Dillwyn and Co.—18th and 19th centuries.

1-23. Early Worcester marks of various workmen employed at the factory. These marks are from 1752 to 1800.

24-28. This mark is believed by experts to be Dr. Wall's mark.

29. Various forms of crescents, which are hard to distinguish from other marks during that time. The mark was usually impressed or gilded, sometimes a blue or gold stamp was used.

30-34. These are early imitations of Chinese marks.

35-41. More fancy imitations of Chinese marks, early date.

42-44. ROBERT HANCOCK'S mark.

45-48. Imitation of the Dresden mark.

49. Imitation of the Sevres mark.

50. Imitation of Chantilly mark.

ALPHABETICAL LIST OF NAMES AND INITIALS FOUND ON ENGLISH WARES.

T.—Staffordshire; 18th century.

T. H. and O.—Uncertain.

Talor, William—Staffordshire; 17th century.

Toft, Ralph—Staffordshire; 17th century.

Toft, Thomas—Staffordshire; 17th century.

Turner — Lane End, Staffordshire; 18th century.

Turner and Co.—Lane End, Staffordshire; 18th century.

Turner's Patent—Lane End, Staffordshire; 18th century.

Turner, Ralf—Staffordshire; 18th century.

Twyford, J.—Staffordshire; 18th century.

Voyez—Hanley, Staffordshire; 18th century.

Voyez, J.—Hanley, Staffordshire; 18th century.

W (* * *).—Leeds, Yorkshire; 18th century.

W. R. and Co. — Etruscan, Staffordshire; 19th century.

W. S. and Co., on Stockton ware; 19th century.

W. T. and Co., on Fulham ware; 18th century.

Wagstaff—Vauxhall; 18th century.

Walton—Staffordshire; 18th century.

Warburton, J.—Staffordshire; 18th century.

Wedgwood—Burslem and Etruria, Staffordshire; 18th century.

Wedgwood, Etruria—Burslem and Etruria, Staffordshire; 18th century.

Wedgwood and Bentley—Burslem and Etruria, Staffordshire; 18th century.

Wedgwood and Bentley, Etruria—Burslem and Etruria, Staffordshire; 18th century.

W. and B. (Wedgwood and Bentley) — Burslem and Etruria, Staffordshire; 18th century.

Wedgwood and Co. — Ferrybridge, near Pontefract; 18th century.

Wedgwood, F.—Stockton; 19th century.

Wedgewood—Stockton; 19th century.

Wilson—Hanley, Staffordshire; 18th century.

Wood, Enoch—Burslem, Staffordshire; 18th century.

Wood, Enoch, and Sons—Burslem, Staffordshire; 19th century.

Wood, Ralph—Burslem, Staffordshire; 18th century.

Wood and Caldwell — Burslem, Staffordshire; 19th century.

Wright, John — Staffordshire; 17th and 18th centuries.

51-53. Mr. Flight purchased the works in 1783. The name FLIGHT was also impressed with the crescent.

54. Mark of Barr of 1793.

55-56. Mark of Flight & Barr, used until 1807.

57-59. Mark used until 1813.

60. Mark used 1813 to 1840.

61. Mark of CHAMBERLAIN, 1788 to 1804.

62. Used by CHAMBERLAIN until 1814.

63. From 1814 to 1820.

64. From 1840 to 1850.

65. After 1847.

66. Mark of KERR & BINNS, 1851.

67. Mark used by KERR & BINNS on special order works.

67A-67B. Late WORCESTER MARKS.

68. STOKE, now known as MINTONS. Established 1790. Mark used on a printed form.

69-70. Early mark imitating the mark of Sevres.

71. Mark used 1868.

72. Mark used before 1848.

73. Mark after 1868.

74-81. Later MINTONS mark after 1868.

82-87. SWANSEA. Either printed or impressed. While the firm's existence dates back to 1700, it really started to make good china in 1802 by Mr. Billengsley, and after several years again made china of less expensive taste.

88. NANTGARROW. 1813 to 1820.

89. LONGPORT (known as Davenport). About 1800.

90. LONGPORT.

91-92. LIVERPOOL.

93-94. LANE DELPH. Various forms of the name MASON used. Later mark of FENTON STONE WORKS, and C. J. M. & CO., either printed or impressed use, established late 18th century.

95. BRIDGWOOD & CLARK, 1857.

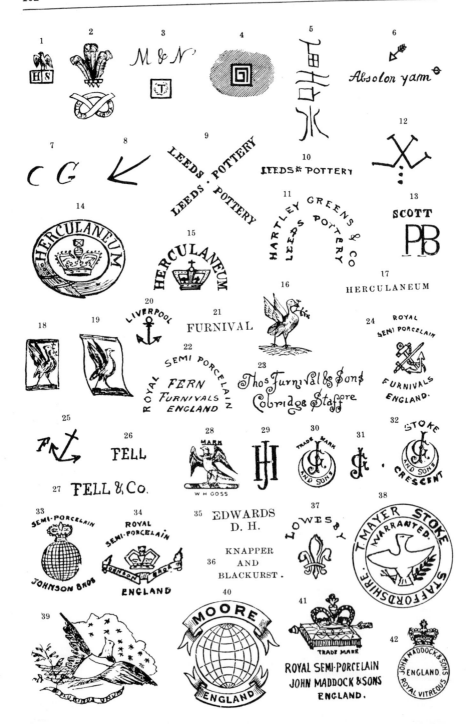

1. LONGTON. Hilditch & Son.

2. TUNSTALL.

3. LONGTON. Manufactured by MAYER & NEWBOLD.

4-5. ELERSWARE.

6. ABSOLON, also known as YARMOUTH, 1788.

7-11. LEEDS. C.G. stands for Charles Green, established 1758. For a time made products which were considered as fine as Wedgwood, most famous are their cream colored wares, their baskets and open work pieces are also considered fine.

12. W. LITTLER. Longton. Established about 1750.

13. EDINBURGH. (Portobello Pottery.)

14-20. HERCULANEUM. Liverpool. Established about 1790, first mark is Herculaneum impressed, other marks in order. Most famous of the Liverpool potteries.

21-24. FURNIVALS. Cobridge.

25-27. FELL & CO. Established 1817. Made similar goods to the Leeds factory. However, they were inferior.

28. G. H. GOSS. Stoke-on-Trent. Made ware called Belleek; all articles were extremely fine, and carefully executed.

29. J. HOLDCROFT. Longton. Majolica ware.

30-32. G. JONES & SONS. Stoke-on-Trent. This firm made fine quality goods in all their products.

33-34. JOHNSON BROS. Established 1883.

35-36. Founded 1800 by Rogers Bros. In 1852 the works were purchased by James Edwards, and then again sold to Knapper & Blackhurst.

37. LOWESBY. 1835.

38-39. T. MAYER. Stoke. Founded about 1830. Specialized in making historical American plates.

40. MOORE BROS. Longton. Very fine ornamental products.

41-42. JOHN MADDOCK & SONS. Burslem. Large factory, and highly successful; established 1830.

1-3. ALFRED MEAKIN, Tunstail. Established 1881.

4-5. I. NEALE, Hanley. 1776. Made good quality wares, imitated Wedgwood styles.

6-7. THE NEW HALL WORKS, 1778-1810.

8-10. OLD HALL WORKS. Established 1790 by Job Meigh. Made a good quality earthenware, and semi-porcelain.

11. Late OLD HALL mark.

12. NEW WHARF POTTERY, Burslem.

13-14. POINTONS, Shelton. Chinaware ad ornamental wares.

15. PITCAIRNS, LTD.

16. PODMORE, WALKER & CO.

17. PINDER BOURNE & CO., later sold to the Doulton Works.

18. POOLE & UNWIN, Longton.

19. J. PENNINGTON. About 1750, Liverpool.

20. PLANT BROS., Longton.

21. H. PALMER. Hanley imitations of Wedgewood.

22-29. RIDGWAYS, Shelton. Established by William, brother of John Ridgway of the Cauldon works.

30-31. JOHN TURNER, Longton. Established 1872.

32. TOOTH & CO. Fine colored lustre wares.

1

E. WOOD & SON BURSLEM.
SEMI CHINA
WARRANTED

2

ENOCH WOOD & SON
BURSLEM.
WOOD & CALDWELL

3

W & Co
CLEMATIS
HANLEY
ENGLAND.

4

5

W & R
STOKE ON TRENT
CARLTON WARE

6

U P
Co
HANLEY
ENGLAND

7

DURABILITY
J. H. W. & SONS.
HANLEY,
ENGLAND

8

ROYAL
SEMI PORCELAIN
WOOD & SON
ENGLAND.

9

ROYAL PATENT IRONSTONE.
ARTHUR J WILKINSON
LATE R. ALCOCK
BURSLEM

10

A. J. WILKINSON & Co
ENGLAND.

11

THE FOLEY CHINA
W
ENGLAND.

12

STAFFORDSHIRE

13

WILKINSON'S
W
ROYAL SEMI PORCELAIN
BURSLEM, ENGLAND.

14

STUBBS & KENT
LONGPORT

15

W. & B. Lto
B

16

TRADE MARK.
B. M & T.

17

18

TRADE MARK
H & C
F

19

S. F. & Co

20

S F & Co
ENGLAND

21

R H P
& Co

22

S & F.

1-2. ENOCH WOOD & SONS, Burslem. Established 1784. Fine china and earthenware, made many historical plates for American trade.

3. WHITTAKER HEATH & CO., Hanley.

4. F. W. WINKLE & CO., Hanley.

5. WILTSHAW & ROBINSON.

6. UPPER HANLEY POTTERY CO., Hanley.

7. J. H. WETHERBY & SONS, Hanley.

8. WOOD & SON, Burslem.

9. A. J. WILKINSON, Burslem.

10. A. J. WILKINSON & CO., Burslem.

11. WILEMAN & CO., Longton. Good chinaware.

12. CROWN STAFFORDSHIRE PORCELAIN CO., Fenton. One of the largest china producing factories of England.

13. WILKINSON'S, Burslem.

14. STUBBS & KENT, Longport.

15. WOOD & BARKER, Burslem.

16. BOULTON MACHIN & TENNANT, Tunstall.

17. T. C. GREEN & CO., Burton.

18. HULME & CHRISTIE, Fenton.

19-20. S. FIELDING & CO., Stoke-on-Trent.

21. R. H. PLANT & CO., Longton.

22. SMITH & FORD, Burslem.

1-10. DOULTON (ROYAL DOULTON). One of the most famous English manufacturers, located at Burslem and Lambeth. This firm makes every type of fine porcelain. Established 1872.

11-24a. WEDGWOOD.

25. SMITH & BINNALL, Tunstall.

26. S. & E. COLLIER, Reading.

27. T. MALLING & SONS, Newcastle on Tyne.

28. SHERWIN & COTTON, Hanley.

29. WEDGWOOD & CO., Tunstall. Established 1768 by Josiah Wedgwood & Thomas Bentley. (See Page 17.)

30. T. & C. GREEN & CO., Greesley.

31. GRIMWADE BROS., Stoke upon Trent.

32. J. HOLDCROFT, Longton.

33. LOCKE & CO., Worcester.

1-3. E. BENNET POTTERY CO., Baltimore. Established about 1840.

4. J. H. BAUM, Wellsville.

5. L. B. BEERBOWER & CO., Elizabeth, N. J.

6. BROCKMAN POTTERY CO., Cincinnati, Ohio. Established 1862.

7-10. BURFORD BROS., East Liverpool, Ohio.

11-12. BURROUGHS & MOUNTFORD, Trenton, N. J. This firm, established 1879, made articles similar in decoration and design to the English Doulton wares. They later became known as The Eagle Pottery Co.

13. THE CHELSEA CHINA CO., New Cumberland. Produced a good quality of china about 1888. Existed about 10 years and went out of business.

14-15. THE CERAMIC ART CO., Trenton, N. J. Better known as Lenox China, started operation in 1879, by Mr. Lenox and Mr. Coxon. From the beginning this firm excelled all others in the quality of their products, and today is among the finest in the world. Their fame is international. Among their first products were pieces made in the style of Belleek, although articles of their own originality, like the lotus leaf pattern, were made.
Mark No. 14 is often confused with the Irish Belleek.

16-19. CHELSEA POTTERY. Also known as CERAMIC ART WORKS. This firm was originally situated in Chelsea, Mass., about 1866, and about 1891 removed to Dedham, Mass.

20. COOK POTTERY CO., Trenton. This factory commenced operations about 1863. In 1876, during the Centennial Exhibition, they displayed numerous busts and figures made of parian, which were immediately successful. The firm also produced a Belleek type ware. Wm. Bromley, who was formerly employed by W. H. Goss, helped model these pieces.

21. U. S. POTTERY, Bennington, Vt.

22-23. FAIENCE MFG. CO., Brooklyn, N. Y. Founded in 1880, made fine decorated vases, also a ware on the order of majolica, copied the lustres of Italy and Spain. These works have since closed.

24-25. THE GLOBE POTTERY CO., E. Liverpool, Ohio.

1-3. THE GREENWOOD POTTERY CO., Trenton, N. J. Commenced operations 1864, and after many experiments, finally made good china.

4-6. THE GOODWIN POTTERY CO., East Liverpool. John Goodwin, formerly employed in England, opened a factory in 1844.

7-10. D. F. HAYES & SON, Baltimore, Md.

11-12. HARKER POTTERY CO., E. Liverpool, Ohio. About 1840.

13-25. THE INTERNATIONAL POTTERY CO., Trenton. Established 1879.

1. J. E. JEFFORDS & CO., Philadelphia, Pa. Established 1868.

2-12. KNOWLES, TAYLOR & KNOWLES & CO., East Liverpool. Established about 1854. Was at one time considered the largest manufacturer in America.

13-16. HOMER LAUGHLIN CHINA CO., East Liverpool, Ohio. Established 1872, made a very high grade porcelain and earthenware.

17-19. MAYER POTTERY CO., Beaver Falls, Pa., Established 1881, by sons of former owner of factories in England.

20. THE LONHUDA POTTERY CO., Steubenville, Ohio. Made products similar to Rookwood.

21. MARYLAND POTTERY CO., Baltimore, Md.

22. MORRIS & WILLMORE, Trenton, N. J. Established by former employees of the Worcester Works, about 1893. Made articles resembling Worcester and Belleek.

23. JOHN MADDOCK & SONS, Trenton, N. J. Made articles resembling Doulton. Established about 1893.

1-4. JERSEY CITY POTTERY COMPANY, Jersey City, N. J. One of the earliest American potteries. Established about 1825.

5-14. JOHN MOSES & SONS, CO., Trenton. Established 1863, one of the first potteries to make articles at popular prices.

15-21. MERCER POTTERY CO., Trenton, N. J. Established 1869.

22-27. NEW ENGLAND POTTERY CO., Boston, Mass. Established 1854.

1. OHIO CHINA CO., E. Palestine, O.

2-7. ONONDAGA POTTERY CO., Syracuse, N. Y. Founded 1871. Made a very fine line of chinawares, and ornaments. Their first mark is a seal of the State of New York.

8-10. OTT & BREWER, Trenton, N. J.

11-18. DRESDEN POTTERY WORKS, also known as (Potters Co-operative Co.). Established 1876.

19-21. PEORIA POTTERY CO., Peoria, Ill.

22. ROOKWOOD. Mrs. Storer founded the Rookwood Works about 1880. This is one of the foremost firms today. Their works have received international fame. Mark up to 1882.

23. These initials stand for ROOKWOOD POTTERY, CINCINNATI, OHIO. MARIA LONGWORTH NICHOLS.

24-29. Marks used up to 1886.

30. Used 1886.

31. One flame indicated 1 year; this is 1887.

32. This indicated 1895.

1. RITTENHOUSE EVANS & CO., Trenton, N. J.

2. THE SEBRING POTTERY CO., E. Liverpool. Established 1887.

3-11. THE STEUBENVILLE POTTERY CO., Steubenville, Ohio. 1879.

12. C. C. THOMPSON POTTERY CO., East Liverpool, Ohio. 1888. Very large factory.

13. TUCKER & HULME, Philadelphia, Pa. Established 1825. Factory was in existence only 10 years.

14. U. S. POTTERY, Bennington, Vt. Established 1846, this firm was the first American firm to produce biscuit figures. Factory closed after 10 years.

15. UNION POTTERY CO., East Liverpool, O.

16-20. UNION PORCELAIN WORKS, Brooklyn, N. Y. Established about 1874.

21-24. VODREY POTTERY CO., East Liverpool, Ohio. Established 1857.

25-28. SAMUEL WELLER, Zanesville, Ohio. Made works resembling that of Rookwood.

29-32. WILLETS MFG. CO., Trenton, N. J. Organized 1853. This firm has made some of the most beautiful of the Belleek wares.

33-36. WARWICK CHINA CO., Wheeling, W. Va. 1887. Large assortment of fine ceramic wares. Very enterprising firm.

37-8. WEST END POTTERY CO., East Liverpool, Ohio. 1893.

39. WICK CHINA CO., Kittanning, Pa.

1-5. WELLSVILLE POTTERY CO., Wellsville, Ohio. 1879.

6-13. WHEELING POTTERY CO., Wheeling, W. Va. 1879.

14. CHITTENANGO POTTERY CO., Chittenango, N. Y. 1897. Made
a fine quality of bone china.

POTTERY AND PORCELAIN MARKS

American ....110 to 123

Denmark, Russia, Poland 86, 87

England ....88 to 109

Flemish 78, 79

France ....38 to 59

Germany, Austria, Hungary ....60 to 77

Holland ....80 to 83

Italy ....22 to 37

Swedish, Spanish, German, Portuguese 84, 85

INDEX

A

Absolon, 102, 103
Adams, (William), 89
Adams, J.
Adderly, Wm. & Co., 92, 93.
Abrenfeldt & Son, 76, 77.
Alcock, J. & G., 92, 93, 94, 95.
Alcora, 84, 85.
Alten-Rothau, 74, 75.
American Plates, 94, 95.
Andreodi, Giorgio, 24, 25.
Amsterdam, 80, 81.
Annaburg, 68, 69.
Anspach, 60, 61, 64, 65.
Aprey, 40, 41.
Arnoldi, 68, 69.
Arnstadt, 64, 65.
Arras, 42, 43, 56, 57.
Ashworth, George & Bros., 92, 93.
Avisseau, 44, 45.
Avon, 38, 39.
Aynsley, J., 89.

B

Baden & Baden, 64, 65.
Baensch, 68, 69.
Baguley, Isaas, 92, 93.
Bailey & Batkin, 89.
Baireuth, 60, 61, 66, 67.
Baquesne, M., 39.
Baranowka, 86, 87.
Barker, S. & Sons, 92, 93.
Bassano, 34, 35.
Bates, Elliott, 94, 95.
Bawo & Dotter, 76, 77.
Baum, J. H., 110, 111.
Beauvais, 38, 39.
Beech, James, 94, 95.
Beerbower, L. B. & Co., 110, 111.
Belleek, 92, 93.
Bellevue, 92, 93.
Benedikt Bros., 68, 69.
Bennette Pottery Co., 110, 111.
Bernart, Jean, 39.
Bertram, Berhard Luftelburg, 68, 69.
Birch, 89.
Bodley, E. J. D., 92, 93.
Bolt & Co., 89.
Booth, Enoch, 89.
Boisette, 56, 57.
Boote, T. & R., 92, 93.
Booths, 94, 95.
Bordeaux, 58, 59.
Bordollo Bros., Grunstadt, 68, 69.
Böttcher, 62, 63.
Bötcher, 62, 63.
Boulton & Machin & Tennant, 106, 107.
Bourg, La Reine, 40, 41, 56, 57.
Bourne, E., 94, 95.
Bournes Potteries, 89.
Bow China Works, 89.
Brameld, 89.

Bramels & Co., 92, 93.
Brancas, Lauragais, 58, 59.
Bridgewood & Clark, 100-101.
Bridgwood & Son, 89.
Bristol, 94, 95.
Brockman Pottery Co., 110, 111.
Brownfield, W. & Son, 94, 95.
Brown, Westhead, Moore & Co., 94, 95.
Bruges, 78, 79.
Brussels, 78, 79.
Buckauer, Porz, 68, 69.
Bulkeley & Bent, 89.
Buen, Retiro, 37, 84, 85.
Burford Bros., 110, 111.
Burroughs & Mountford, 110, 111.

C

C. G., (Charles Green), 89.
Cadogan, 89.
Caffagnolo, 72, 73.
Capo, di Monte, 36, 37.
Carpentier, Francois, 39.
Castel, Durante, 28, 29.
Castelli, 36, 37.
Catherine 2nd of Russia, 46, 47.
Caughley, 89.
Ceramic Art Co., 110, 111.
Chaffers, 92, 92.
Chamberlain, 100, 101.
Champman, 92, 93.
Chantilly, 56, 57, 98, 99.
Charles X, 46, 47.
Charlottenberg, 66, 67.
Chatham & Wooley, 95.
Chelsea, 89.
Chelsea China Co., 110, 111.
Chelsea Pottery, 110, 111.
Child, 89.
Chittenango Pottery Co., 112.
Chmeloff, 86, 87.
Choisy-le-Roi, 58, 59.
Clews, 89.
Cligancourt, 42, 43, 56, 57.
Close & Co., 89.
Coalport, 89.
Cobridge Works, 94, 95.
Cockworthy, W., 96, 97.
Colebrook, Dale, 96, 97.
Collier, S. & E., 108, 109.
Cookson & Harding,
Cook Pottery Co., 110, 111.
Copeland, W. T. & Sons, 96, 97.
Copenhagen, 86, 87.
Cornaro, 34, 35.
Countess Cosel, 62, 63.
Cross, Sworp, 62, 63.
Crawn, Staffordshire Porcelain Co., 106, 107.
Crystal Ware, 89.

D

Daehmel, 68, 69.
Davenport, 92, 93.

INDEX

Dawson, 89.
De Drie Klokken, 80, 81.
De Drie Porceleyne Astonnen, 80, 81.
De Drie Poreleyne Fleschjes, 80, 81.
De Dubbelde Schenkan, 80, 81.
De Griekse, 80, 81.
De Klaauw, 80, 81.
De Lampetkan, 80, 81.
De Porcelein Byl, 80, 81.
De Porcelyene Schootel, 80, 81.
De Poreleyne Fles, 80, 81.
Derby, 90, 91.
De Romeyn, 80, 81.
De Roos, 80, 81.
De Twee Scheepjes, 80, 81.
De Twe Wildemans, 80, 81.
De Vergulde Blompot, 80, 81.
De Witte Ster, 80, 81.
Dillwyn & Co., 89.
Diruta, 30, 31.
Dixon, Austin,& Co., 89.
Don Pottery, 89.
Doulton (Royal Doulton), 108, 109.
Dresden, 62, 63, 98, 99, 118, 119.
Dudson, 91.
Duke of Orleans, 42, 43.
Dwenger, 76, 77.
De Witte Ster, 80, 81.
Dwight, J., 91.

E

Eagle Pottery Co., 110, 111.
Early French Porcelain, 56, 57, 58.
Early Mark Meissener Porzellan
    Manufacture, 62, 63.
Eastwood, 91.
Edinburgh, 102, 103.
Edwards, J., 92, 93.
Eisenberger, 68, 69.
Elersware, 102, 103.
Empress Catherine, 86, 87.

F

F. G., 91.
Fabriana, 30, 31.
Faenza, 30, 31, 32, 33.
Faience Mfg. Co., 110, 111.
Fell & Co., 91, 102, 103.
Fenton Stone Works, 100, 101.
Fiegel, F. G., 65.
Fielding, S. & Co., 106, 107.
Flight, 100, 101.
Flight & Barr, 100, 101.
Fontainebleau, 56, 57.
Forli, Master Jeronimo, 32, 33.
France, Marks of France, 38, 39, 50, 51,
    52, 53, 54, 55.
Franke, A., 68, 69.
Frankenthal, 60, 61, 66, 67.
Freeling & Co., 91.
Fulda, 62, 63.
Fulham Pottery, 91.
Furnivals, 102, 103.
Furstenberg, 62, 63.

G

G. Green, 91.
Gardner, 86, 87.
Genoa, 34, 35.
Gera, 64, 65.
Ginori, Marquis, 36, 37.
Giustini Brothers, 36, 37.
Globe Pottery Co., 110, 111.
Goggingen, 60, 61.
Goodwin Pottery Co., 112, 113.
Goss, G. H., 102, 103.
Gotha, 62, 63, 72, 73.
Gottskowski, 67.
Green, Charles, 102, 103.
Green, Stephen, 91.
Green, T. C., 106, 107, 108, 109.
Greenwood Pottery Co., 112, 113.
Greiner, G., 65.
Greinstadt, 67.
Grimwade Brothers, 108, 109.
Grosbreitenbach, 64, 65.
Grue, 37.
Gubbio, 24, 25, 26, 27.
Gunther & Co., S. B. B., 91.

H

H. & S., 91.
Hackwood, 91.
Hamburger & Co., 76, 77.
Hancock, Robert, 98, 99.
Hannong, Paul, 61.
Harburg, 60, 61.
Harker Pottery Co., 112, 113.
Harding, 91.
Harley, T., 91.
Harrison, G., 91.
Hartley, Greens & Co., 91.
Hayes, D. F. & Sons, 112, 113.
Heath, 91.
Herculaneum, 91, 102, 103.
Herend, 74, 75.
Hesse, Cassel, 62, 63.
Hesse, Darmstadt, 62, 63.
Hildescheim, 64, 65.
Hochst, 60, 61.
Holdcroft, 102, 103, 108, 109.
Homer Laughlin China Co., 114, 115.
Hubbe Brothers, 70, 71.
Hulme & Christie, 106, 107.
Hussl, J., 70, 71.
Hutschendreuther, C. M., 70, 71.
Hollins, S., 91.
Hollins, T. and J., 91.

I

I. E. B., 91.
In Der Vergulde Boor, 80, 81.
International Pottery Co., 112, 113.
In Toude Moriaans Hofft, 80, 81.

J

Jackson, G., 70, 71.
Jacobi, Adler & Co., 70, 71.

INDEX

Jeffords, J. E. & Co., 114, 115.
Jersey City Pottery Co., 116, 117.
Jobson, 91.
Johnson Brothers, 102, 103.
Jones, G. & Sons, 102, 103.

K

Keeling, J., 91.
Keller & Guerin, 43.
Kerr & Binns, 100, 101.
Kiel, 84, 85.
Kiev, 86, 87.
Kings Period, 62, 63.
Koniglich Bayerische Porz, 70, 71.
Koos, Max, 70, 71.
Korniloff Brothers, 86, 87.
Korzec, 86, 87.
Krause, R., 70, 71.
Krister, C., 70, 71.
Kunersberg, 84, 85.

L

Lakin, 91.
Lakin & Poole, 91.
Lane, Delph, 100, 101.
La Sienie, 56, 57.
La Tour D'aigues, 44, 45, 56, 57.
Leeds, C. G., 102, 103.
Leeds Pottery, 91.
Liege, 78, 79.
Lille, 40, 41, 57, 58, 59.
Limbach, 64, 65.
Limoges, 44, 45, 48, 49.
Littler, W., 102, 103.
Liverpool, 100, 101.
Locke, 108, 109.
Lockett, J. 91.
Lodi, 34, 35.
Longport, 100, 101.
Longton, 102, 103.
Lonhuda Pottery Co., 114, 115.
Lowesby,
Louis XVIII, 46, 47.
Louis Phillipe, 46, 47.
Lowesby, 102, 103.
Ludwigsburg, 64, 65.
Luneville, 42, 43.
Luxembourg Boch Brothers, 78, 79.

M

Macheleidt, 64, 65.
Maddock, John Sons, 102, 103, 114, 115.
Madgeburg, Nuestadt, 68, 69.
Makers of Delft Pottery, 80, 81.
Malines, 78, 79.
Malling, T. & Sons, 108, 109.
Manufacture De Porcelaine De France, 47.
Marans, 42, 43.
Marieberg, 84, 85.
Mark of Louis XVIII.
Marseilles, 42, 43, 58, 59, 70, 71.

Marshall & Co., 91.
Maryland Pottery Co., 114, 115.
Mason, M., 91.
Mason's Paten Iron-stone China, 91.
Mason's Cambrian Argil, 91.
Mason, 100, 101.
Mathault, 40, 41.
Maurienne, 34, 35.
Mayer, E., Hanley, 91.
Mayer & Newbold, 91.
Mayer Pottery Co., 114, 115.
Mayer, T., 102, 103.
Maekin, Alfred, 104, 105.
Medici, Francesco de Medici, 26, 27.
Meigh, 93.
Meigh, J., and Sons, 93.
Meillonas, 40, 41.
Meissen, 62, 63.
Mennecy, 40, 41.
Mennecy, Villeroy, 56, 57.
Mercer Pottery Co., 116, 117.
Mettlach, 77.
Milan, 34, 35.
Miles, Thomas, 93.
Milson, 93.
Minton & Boyle,
Mintons, 100, 101.
Miscellaneous Marks, German Porcelain, 68, 69.
Miscellaneous Marks, Late Austrian & German Porcelain, 70, 71.
Mist, London, 95.
Moore & Co., 95.
Monte, Lupo, 24, 25.
Moore Brothers, 102, 103.
Morris & Willmore, 114, 115.
Mortlock, 93.
Moscow, 86, 87.
Moseley, 95.
Moses, John & Sons, 116, 117.
Moustiers, 40, 41, 42, 43.
Myat, T., 95.

N

Nantgarrow, 100, 101.
Naples, 36, 37.
Neale & Co., 95.
Neale & Wilson, 95.
Neale, Hanley, 95, 104, 105.
Neeld, 95.
Nell, 95.
Nevers, 44, 45.
New England Pottery Co., 116, 117.
Newcastle, 95.
New Hall Works, 104, 105.
New Wharf Pottery, 104, 105.
Nichols, Maria Longworth, 118, 119.
Niderviller, 40, 41, 58, 59.
Norddeutche Steinguttfabrik, 68, 69.
Nove, 34, 35.
Nurembuerg, 60, 61.
Nymphenberg, 66, 67.

INDEX

O

Ohios China Co., 118, 119.
Oiron, 38, 39.
Old Hall Works, 104, 105.
Onondaga Pottery Co., 118, 119.
Opaque Porcelain, 95.
Orleans, 56, 57, 58, 59.
Ott & Brewer, 118, 119.

P

Padua, 34, 35.
Palmer & Neale, 95.
Palmer & Voyeb, 95.
Palmer, 104, 105.
Paris, 41, 42, 43, 56, 57, 58, 59.
Pearlware, 95
Pennington, 104, 105.
Peoria Pottery Co., 118, 119.
Pepovecki, 72, 73.
Pesaro, 34, 35, 36, 37.
Phillips, E., 97.
Pinder, Bourne & Co., 104, 105.
Pinxton, 96, 97.
Pisa, 24, 25.
Pitcairns, Ltd., 104, 105.
Plant, B., 97.
Plant Brothers, 104, 105.
Plant, R. H., 106, 107.
Podmore, Walker & Co., 104, 105.
Pointons, 104, 105.
Poole, R., 97.
Poole & Unwin, 104, 105.
Poppelsdorf, 60, 61.
Porcelaine De Monsievr, 42, 43.
Portuguese Marks, 84, 85.
Porzellan Fabrik Kloesterle, 76, 77.
Poterat, A., 38, 39.
Poterat, Louis, 39.
Prague, 74, 75.
Pratt, F. and R. & Co., 97.
Premieres, 40, 41.
Prince of Schwarzburg, 65.
Pulinx, Henri, 78, 79.

Q

Queensware, 31, 37.

R

Rauenstein, 64, 64.
Ravenna, 32, 33.
Regensburg, 66, 67.
Reissberger & Co., 72, 73.
Renac, 42, 43.
Rennes, 43.
Republican Period, 46, 47.
Richus & Toft, 97
Riley's Semi-china, 97.
Ridgways, 97, 104, 105.
Rimini, 32, 33.
Rissler & Co., 72, 73.
Rittenhouse, Evens & Co., 120, 121.
Rockingham, Caogans, 93, 97.
Rogers, 97.

Rome, 30, 31.
Rookwood, 118, 119.
Rorstrand, 84, 85.
Rosenfeld, Lazarus, 70, 71.
Rothenber, 72, 73.
Roussencq, Jean Pierre, 43.
Royal, Berlin, 66, 67.
Royal, Bonn, 70, 71.
Royal, St. Petersburg, 86, 87.
Rudolstadt, 64, 65.

S

Sadler, 97.
Sadler & Green, 97.
Salopian, C., Coalport, 87, 97.
Salt, Staffordshire, 97.
Sales, Prices, 20, 21.
Saltzer, A., 72, 73.
Sampson, Bridgewood & Son, 94, 95.
Sans, William, 97.
Sarreguemines, 40, 41, 42, 43.
Savona, 34, 35.
Sceaux, 40, 41, 42, 43, 56, 57.
Schaaf, Carl, 72, 73.
Shakenwald, 74, 75.
Schaper, Johann, 61.
Schmidt, Albert, 72, 73.
Schmidt & Gebruder, 72, 73.
Schmidt, H., 72, 73.
Schreitzheim, 60, 61.
Scott, 97.
Sewell, 97.
Sewells & Co., 97.
Sharpe, 97.
Shelton, 96, 97.
Sherwin & Cotton, 108, 109.
Shore, J., 97.
Shorthose & Co., 97.
Shorthose & Heath, 97.
Sibury & Bridgwood, 97.
Siena, 24, 25.
Sinceny, 40, 41.
Smith & Binnell.
Smith & Ford, 106, 107.
Sneyd, T., 97.
Snitzer, 97.
Springer & Co., 72, 73.
Sebring Pottery Co., 120, 121.
Seville, 84, 85.
Sevres, 46, 47, 50, 51, 52, 53, 54, 55, 98, 99, 100, 101.
Sewell & Donkin, 97.
Spode (See Copeland), 97.
Stamand Les Eaux, 40, 41.
St. Cloud, 40, 41, 56, 57.
Steel, 97.
Stephenson, A., 97.
Steiner & Adler, 72, 73.
Stralsund, 60, 61.
Strauss, L. & Sons, 70, 71.
Strassbourg, 40, 41, 58, 59.
Stubbs & Kent, 106, 107.
Stubenville Pottery Co., 120, 121.

INDEX

Swansea, 100, 101.
Swansea, Dilwyn & Co., **97.**
Swedish Mark, 84, 85.

T

Talor, William, 99.
Taverne, **40, 41.**
Teplitz, 74, 75.
Tervueren, 78, 79.
Thieme, Carl, 72, 73.
Thiriot, Louis, 72, 73.
Thompson Pottery Co., 120, 121.
T'Hart, 80, 81.
Tillowitz, 68, 69.
T'Jognue, Moriaans Hofft, 80, 81.
Toft, Thomas, 99.
Toft, Ralph, 99.
Tooth & Co., 104, 105.
Tournay, 78, 79.
Treviso, 34, 35.
Tucker & Hulme, 120, 121.
Tunstall, 102, 103.
Ture De Porcelain, 46, 47.
Turin, 34, 35.
Turner, John, 104, 105.
Turner & Co., 99.
Turner, Ralf, 99.
Twyford, J., 99.

U

Union Porcelain Co., 120, 121.
Union Pottery, 120, 121.
Unknown Marks, 24, 25, 48, 49, 50, 61, 66, 67, 68, 69, 70, 71, 74, 75, 78, 79, 82, 83, 84, 85.
Upper Hanley Pottery Co., 106, 107.
Urbino, 28, 29.
U. S. Pottery, 110, 111, 120, 121.
Utzchneider, Paul, 43, 74, 75.

V

Valenciennes, 40, 41, 42, 43, 58, 59.
Vargas, 40, 41.
Venice, 34, 35.
Verona, 34, 35.
Verneulle, 59.
Villeroy & Boch, 76, 77.
Vinvennes, 46, 47, 58, 59.
Vincennes (early Serves), 56, 57.

Vista Algre, 84, 85.
Vodrey Pottery Co., 120, 121.
Von Schwartz, J., 72, 73.
Vordex Pottery Co., 120, 121.
Voyez, 99.
Voyez, J., 99.

W

W, 99.
W. R. & Co., 99.
W. S. & Co., 99.
Wagstaff, 99.
Wallendorf, 64, 65.
Warburton, J., 99.
Warwick China Co., 120, 121.
Wegwood, 108, 109.
Wegeley, W., 67.
Weller, Samuel, 120, 121.
Wellsville Pottery Co., 122, 123.
Wessell, Ludwig, 74, 75.
West End Pottery, 120, 121.
Wetherby, J. H., & Sons, 106, 107.
Wheeling Pottery Co., 122.
Whittaker, Heath & Co., 106, 107.
Wick China Co., 120, 121.
Wileman & Co., 106, 107.
Wilkinson, A. J., 106, 107.
Willets Mfg. Co., **120, 121.**
Wilson, 99.
Wiltshaw & Robinson, 106, 107.
Winkle, F. W., 106, 107.
Wintergurst, 60, 61.
Witteburg, 72, 73.
Wittenberger, 74, 75.
Wood & Barker, 106, 107.
Wood, Enoch & Sons, 106, 107.
Worcester, 98, 99, 100, 101.
Wood & Caldwell, 99.
Wood, Ralph, 99.
Wright, John, 99.
Wurtzburg, 66, 67.

Y

Yarmouth, 102, 103.
Yates & Co., 91.

Z

Zsolnay, 74, 75.
Zurich, 78, 79.